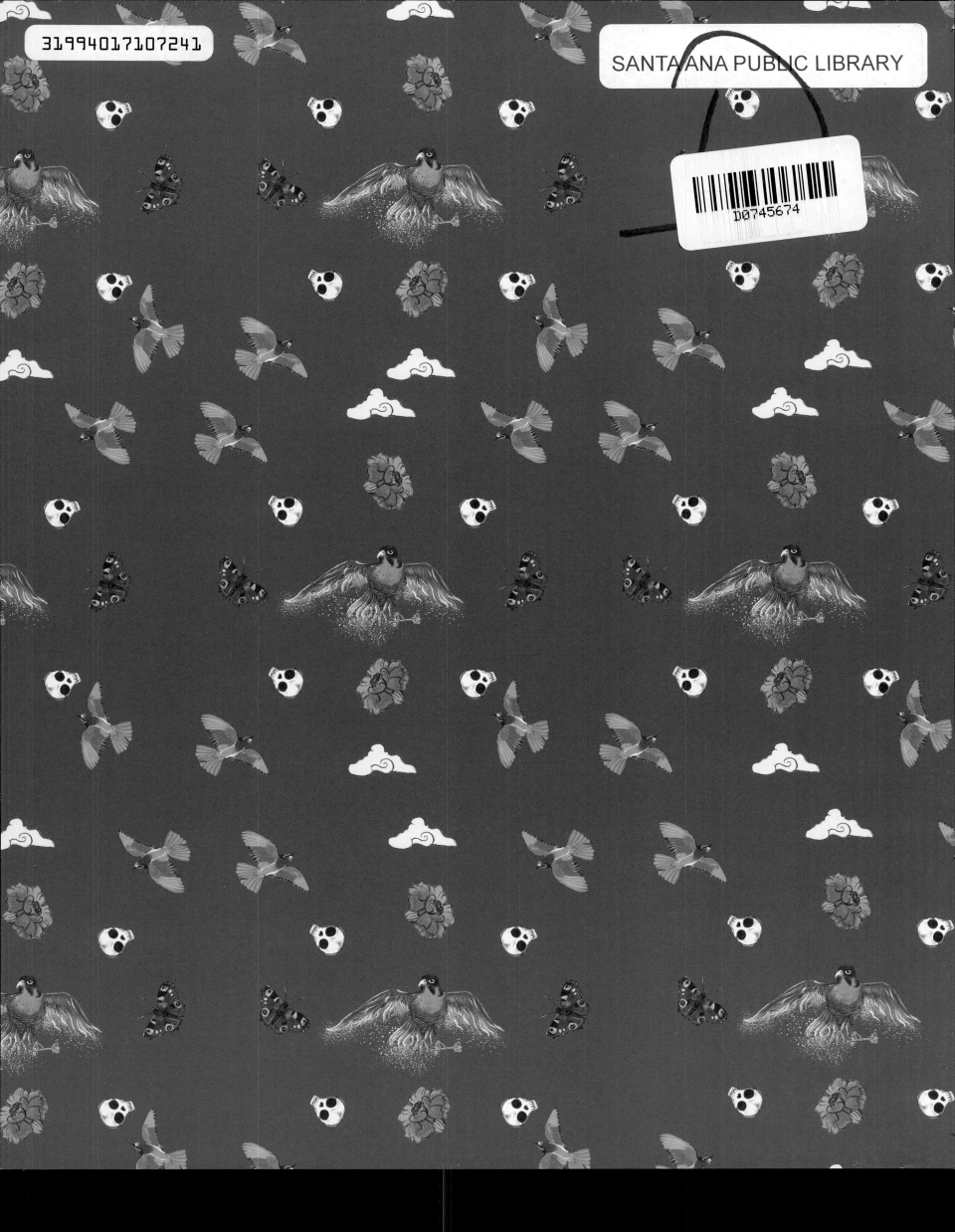

For Joanie and Tess, with all my love. E.H.

To Charcoal, the dog, who reminds me
life could be simple and beautiful. M.

An Atlas of Afterlives © 2023 Quarto Publishing plc.
Text © 2023 Emily Hawkins
Illustrations © 2023 Manasawii

First published in 2023 by Wide Eyed Editions, an imprint of The Quarto Group.
100 Cummings Center, Suite 265D, Beverly, MA 01915, USA.
T +1 978-282-9590 www.Quarto.com

A CIP record for this book is available from the Library of Congress.

ISBN 978-0-7112-8086-1
eISBN 978-0-7112-8088-5

The illustrations were created digitally.
Set in Bruce Standard and Quicksand

Published by Debbie Foy
Designed by Holly Jolley
Commissioned and edited by Alex Hithersay
Production by Dawn Cameron

Manufactured in Malaysia CO062023

9 8 7 6 5 4 3 2 1

Written by Emily Hawkins   Illustrated by Manasawii

An Atlas of Afterlives

Discover Underworlds, Otherworlds and Heavenly Realms

WIDE EYED EDITIONS

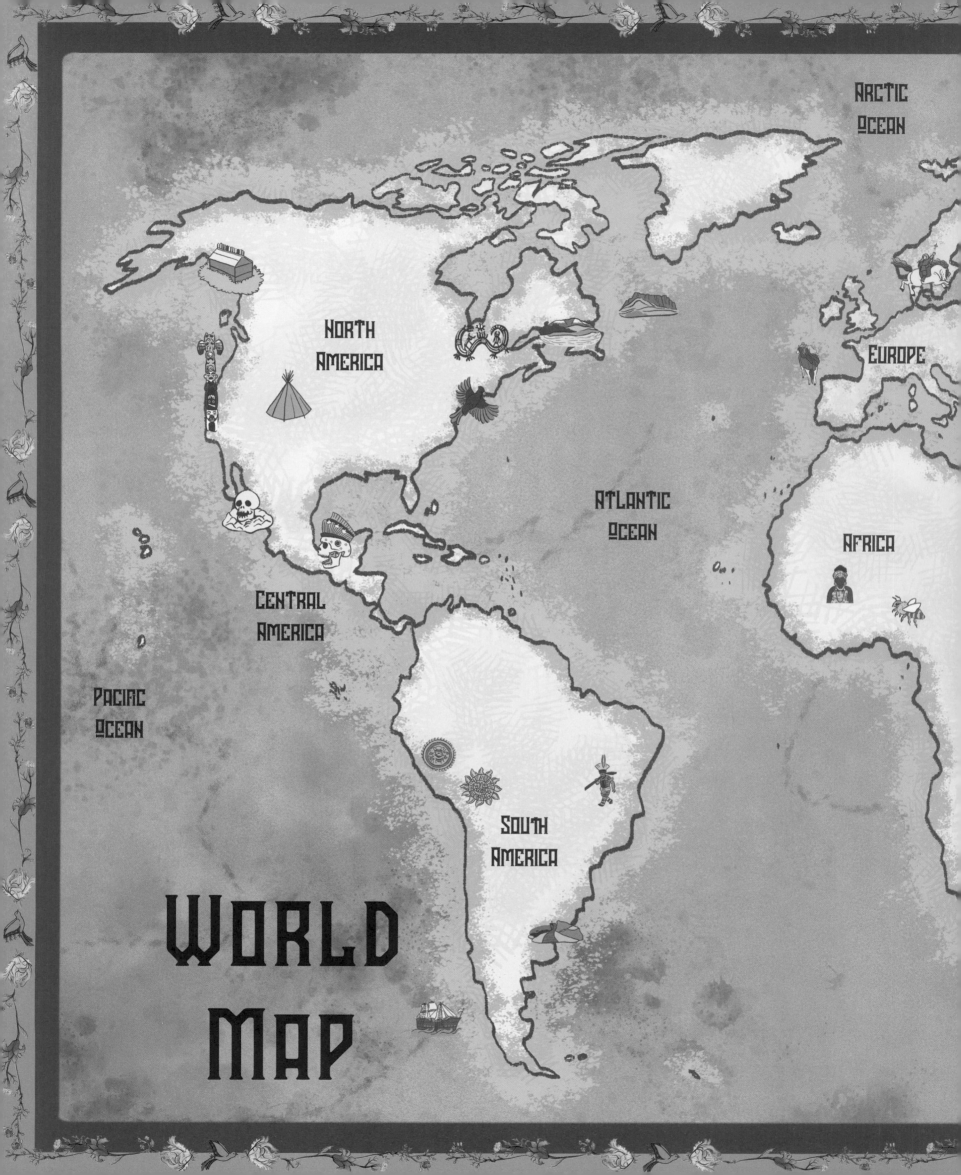

ARCTIC
OCEAN

NORTH
AMERICA

EUROPE

ATLANTIC
OCEAN

AFRICA

CENTRAL
AMERICA

PACIAC
OCEAN

SOUTH
AMERICA

WORLD
MAP

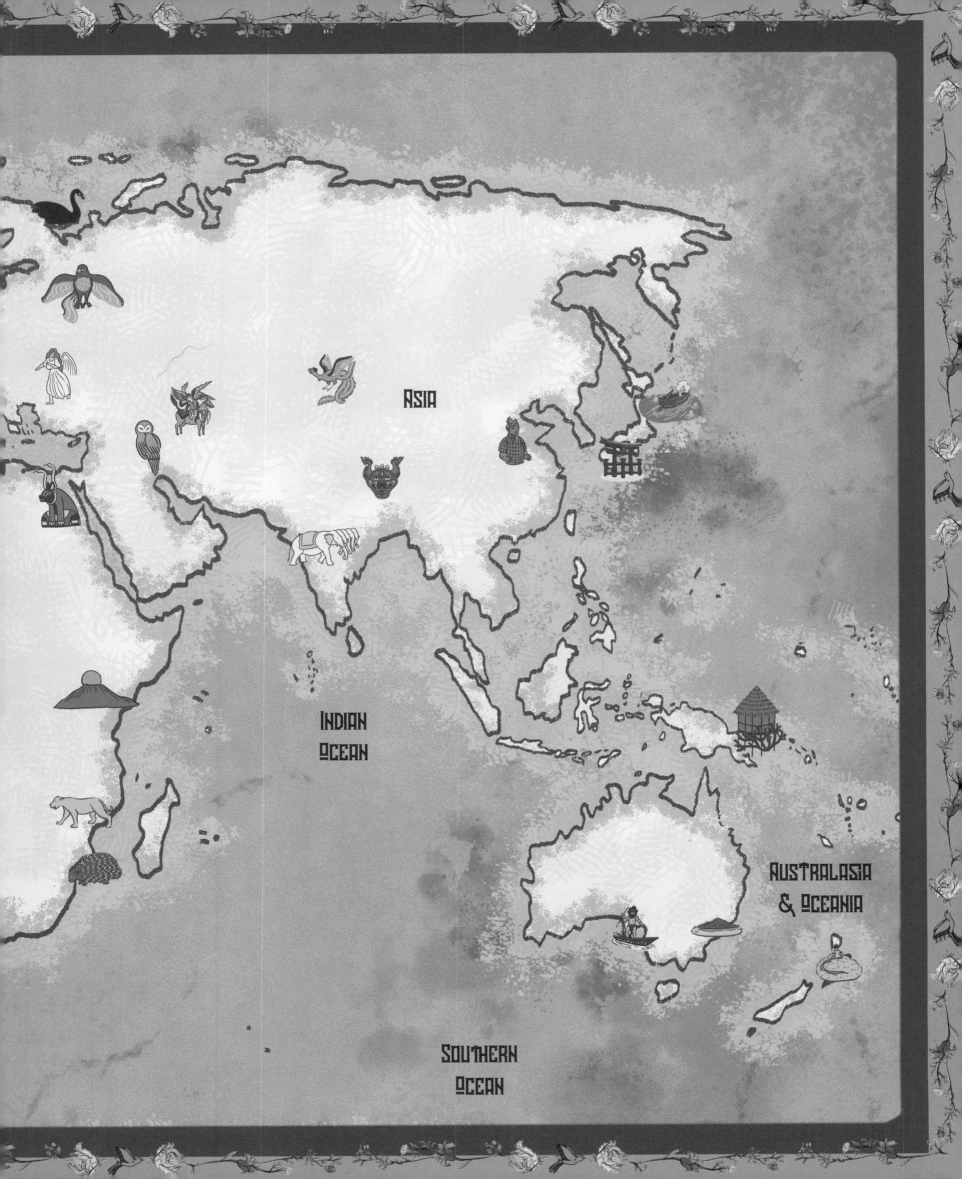

ASIA

INDIAN
OCEAN

AUSTRALASIA
& OCEANIA

SOUTHERN
OCEAN

CONTENTS

10-11   INTRODUCTION

12-13   EUROPE
14-15   HADES The Ancient Greek Underworld
16-17   VALHALLA Hall of the Slain
18-19   VYRAJ Paradise Garden Beyond the Rising Sun
20-21   JACOB'S LADDER Stairway to the Christian Heaven
22-23   THE GATES OF HELL Fiery Portal to the Medieval Underworld
24-25   THE OTHERWORLD Dreamlike Fairyland from Celtic Myths
26-27   THE BAG NOZ Ghostly Ship of Souls
28-29   THE WILD HUNT Phantom Riders of the Night

30-31   AFRICA
32-33   DUAT The Ancient Egyptian Underworld
34-35   THE KALUNGA LINE Boundary Between Worlds
36-37   THE ZULU UNDERWORLD Uncama's Adventures in Underland
38-39   ASAMANDO Ashanti Land of the Dead

40-41   ASIA
42-43   IRKALLA The First Underworld
44-45   UÇMAG AND TAMAG Above and Below
46-47   JANNAH Islamic Paradise Garden
48-49   SVARGA Among the Seven Heavens
50-51   THE BUDDHIST UNDERWORLD Home of Yama, God of Death

52-53 THE TERRACOTTA ARMY Guardians for the Afterlife

54-55 THE CHINVAT BRIDGE Perilous Route to Heaven

56-57 KAKURIYO Hidden World of Spirits

58-59 NORTH AMERICA

60-61 THE TRAIL OF SPIRITS Skyway Through the Stars

62-63 KOTHLUWALAWA Dance-hall of the Dead

64-65 ADLIVUN Watery Underworld of the Inuit People

66-67 THE GATES OF GUINEE Portal to the Voudou Underworld

68-69 MICTLAN The Aztec Underworld

70-71 CENTRAL & SOUTH AMERICA

72-73 XIBALBA The Maya Underworld

74-75 EL CALEUCHE Enchanted Ship of the Dead

76-77 HEDU The Yanomami Heaven

78-79 THREE PACHAS The Worlds of the Incas

80-81 AUSTRALASIA & OCEANIA

82-83 KIBU Island of Ghosts

84-85 HIYOYOA Underwater Gardens of the Dead

86-87 LUA-O-MILU The Hawaiian Land of the Dead

88-89 AFTERWORD

90-91 GLOSSARY and BOOKS THAT HAVE INSPIRED US

92-93 INDEX

You are about to embark on a journey into the unknown...

People have always been fascinated by the mystery of what happens after we die. Is there life after death? And if so, where, exactly, do we go? This book explores the many ways people have tried to answer these questions throughout history and across the globe. This is a guide to otherworldly realms for curious explorers. Within these pages, you will discover heavens, hells, and the places in between: from paradise gardens to fiery underworlds, from shadowy isles of the dead to ghostly galleons on an eternal voyage.

Of course, there is no simple answer to the question of what happens after death. Even within a single religion, people have many different beliefs about the afterlife, and we could never hope to present them all here. But we believe that the places explored in these pages—these glimpses of eternity—are captivating, vibrant examples of spirituality and human creativity. Really, this isn't a book about death at all. It's a book about stories: the stories people have told through the ages to make sense of the world, to make sense of death, and to give comfort and hope.

Journey to the Afterlife

The idea that we might live on in some way after death is
part of many religions and cultures. Some people believe that each
of us has a soul or spirit—which can be described as our personality and
emotions, our thinking and feeling self—which is separate from the physical body.
Most religions teach that a person's soul continues to exist after death, often traveling
to another realm. In this book, we will explore some of these many realms of the afterlife,
as well as various ways of getting there, from magical bridges to supernatural boats, from
heavenly ladders to pathways through the stars.

Locating the Lands of the Dead

Throughout history, humans have envisioned a
multitude of destinations for departing spirits: lands of the
dead were often said to lie under the ground, among the clouds, or on
distant islands across the sea. This book contains maps of each continent
revealing these underworlds, otherworlds, and heavenly realms, as well as some
real-life places with links to the afterlife. For example, there are many tales
of mysterious underworlds that can be reached through caves or the
mouths of fiery volcanoes. These maps are not entirely "real"
in terms of geography, but they reveal a world of
extraordinary stories.

HEKLA VOLCANO: Also known as "Hell's Chimney"

ICELAND

VALHALLA: Hall of the slain

SWEDEN

NORWAY

ST PATRICK'S PURGATORY: Portal to the underworld in medieval Irish myth

THE OTHERWORLD: Dreamlike fairyland from Celtic myth

ATLANTIC OCEAN

ARCTIC OCEAN

IRELAND

GREAT BRITAIN

THE WILD HUNT: Phantom riders of the night

GERMANY

PARIS CATACOMBS: Tunnels storing millions of skeletons

FRANCE

THE BAG NOZ: Ghostly ship of souls from Breton folklore

EUROPE

From the shadowy underworld of Hades—the ancient Greek land of the dead—to the golden mead halls of Viking Valhalla, the myths of Europe offer some captivating visions of the afterlife. Long ago, people believed that it may be possible to reach some of these legendary places through gateways or portals in the real world: the mouths of caves, the craters of volcanoes, or the majestic peaks of snow-capped mountains.

SPAIN

ITALY

MOUNT TEIDE: In Guanche legend, this volcano is the gateway to the home of the demon Guayota

THE GATES OF HELL: Fiery portal to the medieval underworld

TUONELA: Land of the dead in Finnish mythology

FINLAND

RUSSIA

CEAHLAU MASSIF: Home of Zalmoxis, god of death in Romanian folklore

VYRAJ: Slavic paradise garden

UKRAINE

ROMANIA

TURKEY

GREECE

HADES: The ancient Greek underworld

JACOB'S LADDER: Stairway to the Christian Heaven

HADES: THE ANCIENT GREEK UNDERWORLD

Welcome to the underworld. This is the Kingdom of Shadows, where the souls of the departed go to spend a gloomy—or glorious—eternity. The ancient Greeks believed that when someone died, their spirit traveled underground to the land of the dead. To get there, they had to cross the River Styx, which marked the boundary between the world of the living and the kingdom of death. The grim-faced lord of this dark realm shared a name with his kingdom: Hades. He was also known as Pluto, and as Polydegmon, which means "receiver of many guests."

Hades had other rivers as well as the Styx: Acheron, Cocytus, Phlegethon, and Lethe.

Some ancient Greeks believed that portals to the underworld could be found at these places.

NECROMANTEION OF ACHERON

GREECE

CAPE MATAPAN

LERNA

14

RELUCTANT QUEEN

Persephone was the daughter of Demeter, goddess of the harvest. One day, while gathering flowers, Persephone was kidnapped by Hades. He dragged her to his underground kingdom to be his bride. Demeter was furious. While she grieved for her daughter, nothing grew and people went hungry. At last, the king of the gods, Zeus, ordered Hades to release Persephone... as long as she had not eaten anything in the underworld. But Hades had tricked her into swallowing six pomegranate seeds. For the ancient Greeks, this explained fall and winter: for six months every year, Persephone was forced to return to the underworld, and the land fell barren while Demeter wept.

CROSSING THE RIVER

In ancient Greece it was important to give the dead a proper funeral, so that their spirit could reach the underworld instead of wandering forever on the desolate banks of the Styx. The river could only be crossed with help from a ragged ferryman named Charon. The dead were buried with a coin in their mouth to pay Charon's toll, and a honey cake to feed to the hell-hound Cerberus, who guarded the gates of Hades.

PARADISE OR PUNISHMENT?

Most souls that arrived in Hades were sent to the dull plains of Asphodel, but the virtuous spent eternity in the beautiful Elysian Fields. The wicked were condemned to a hellish place called Tartarus. One such soul—King Tantalus—was imprisoned forever in a shallow pool of water below a fruit tree. He was hungry and thirsty, but he could never quite reach the fruit or sip the water. (This is where we get the word "tantalizing," describing a temptation that is just out of reach.) Another man, Sisyphus, was made to push a boulder up a hill, only for it to roll down every time he neared the top.

The three-headed dog Cerberus watched over the gateway to the underworld, preventing the dead from escaping.

VALHALLA: HALL OF THE SLAIN

If you long for an eternity of fighting and feasting, then Valhalla—the Viking hall of the slain—is the place for you. The Vikings were fierce seafaring warriors from Scandinavia who raided the coasts of northern Europe between the ninth and eleventh centuries. Some Vikings believed that if you died a valiant death in combat, your spirit would be taken to Valhalla, home of the great god Odin. This vast, majestic banqueting hall had gleaming walls of gold and a roof made from brightly polished shields. Every day, the heroes of Valhalla rode out to battle each other. As dusk fell, their wounds miraculously healed, and they returned to Odin's hall for a night of feasting before doing it all again the next day.

Odin was king of the Norse gods. He was accompanied by two ravens, and rode an eight-legged horse named Sleipnir.

THE VALKYRIES

Above the Viking battlefields, so the legends say, the Valkyries patrolled the skies, choosing who would die and accompany them to Valhalla. These formidable female warriors were the shield-maidens of Odin.

At Valhalla, Odin kept the best warriors ready for the great war at the end of time: Ragnarok.

The Vikings came from Scandinavia, an area that includes modern-day Norway, Sweden, and Denmark.

The goat Heidrun produced endless honey wine, or mead, for the warriors of Valhalla.

PREPARING FOR THE AFTERLIFE

The Vikings believed that the dead took their possessions with them to the afterlife. Sometimes, when a wealthy person died, their body, dressed in armor and fine clothing, was laid in a ship with weapons, jewelry, food, and drink. Occasionally dogs and horses were killed and placed beside their owners. Then, these ships were either buried in an earthen mound or set alight in a funeral pyre.

HEL, LAND OF THE DEAD

For the people of the Northlands, where you went after death didn't depend on how good or bad you were while alive. Only the most heroic warriors were destined for Valhalla; other people ended up in an underworld called Hel, presided over by a gloomy giantess of the same name. This Hel was not a frightening, fiery pit like the Christian Hell (see page 22). Here, the dead might live on, eating and drinking, fighting and sleeping, just as they did in life.

Valhalla's cook made tasty stews from the meat of a magic boar. Each day, the boar came back to life, to be eaten again!

VYRAJ: PARADISE GARDEN BEYOND THE RISING SUN

Far to the east, beyond the rising sun, lies the beautiful garden of Vyraj, according to Slavic mythology. The Slavic people had many different beliefs about the afterlife. One was that when somebody died, their soul departed to this paradise. Vyraj—also known as Iriy or Rai—was a place of warmth and sunshine, with leafy trees laden with golden fruits. The air was filled with sweet songs from the birds that flew there every winter. When they returned to the living world, they brought the season of spring with them.

Storks were seen as guides between the worlds of the living and the dead. It was bad luck to harm one.

CIRCLE OF LIFE

Some Slavic people believed that after death, a person's soul passed into the body of a bird—often a stork or a nightjar—and began a journey of forty days to reach Vyraj. There the bird would stay, basking in the sunny garden, until the time came to return to the land of the living when a new child was born. The soul would pass to the baby, continuing the circle of life. In this way, many felt that the souls of their ancestors were never truly gone.

The Slavic people originally came from a region including modern-day Ukraine, Belarus, Poland, and several other Eastern and South-Eastern European countries.

SLAVIC REGIONS OF EASTERN AND SOUTH-EASTERN EUROPE:

BELARUS
POLAND
RUSSIA
UKRAINE

In the *World Tree* lived two bird-women: the Alkonost and the Sirin.

Their songs caused forgetfulness in all who heard them.

The gates to Vyraj were guarded by a raróg: a flame-winged falcon that clutched the key in its talons.

World Tree

Some said that in Vyraj grew the enormous, sacred World Tree, which connected all parts of the universe. In other versions of the story, the World Tree did not grow in the garden, but the garden itself was in the canopy of the tree. Others said that the land of the dead lay around the roots of the World Tree.

JACOB'S LADDER: STAIRWAY TO THE CHRISTIAN HEAVEN

Throughout history, people have depicted heaven in many different ways. From the Christian tradition comes the idea of Heaven as a place above the clouds, where the souls of the dead go to be with God. It is seen as a beautiful, peaceful place of eternal rest, bathed in radiant sunbeams. In stories and paintings from medieval Europe, the way to Heaven was often shown as a great ladder or staircase reaching toward the sky. This idea is based on the Bible story of Jacob's Ladder.

DREAMING OF HEAVEN

Genesis, the first book of the Hebrew and Christian Bibles, tells the story of Jacob, who was traveling through the desert. One night, he lay down to rest on the hard ground, using a rock for a pillow. He dreamed of a huge ladder reaching toward Heaven, with angels moving up and down. In some versions of the story, God stands at the top.

In medieval times, many Christians believed that the wonders of Heaven were beyond words and beyond human understanding.

BEYOND THE STARS

Dante Alighieri was an Italian writer from the fourteenth century. In a famous poem called *Paradiso*, he describes a vision of God in Heaven as a brilliant point of light surrounded by nine dazzling, whirling circles of angels. God was thought to reside at the farthest reaches of the universe, beyond the stars.

CELESTIAL CITY

At the end of the Christian Bible, the Book of Revelation paints a detailed picture of Heaven. It describes God sitting on an emerald throne, surrounded by a rainbow and a host of angels. A dazzling city is depicted, built from precious stones, with streets of gold and gates made from pearls. It is said to be shaped like a cube, with each side measuring 12,000 furlongs (1,500 miles). In this celestial city, we are told, there is no death, no sorrow, and no pain.

Today, some Christians believe that Heaven is not a physical place, but a state of being that follows death, where the souls of people come close to God.

THE GATES OF HELL: FIERY PORTAL TO THE MEDIEVAL UNDERWORLD

"Abandon all hope, ye who enter here." In his poem *Inferno*, the fourteenth-century Italian writer Dante imagines a journey into the underworld, where he reads these doom-laden words as he passes through the Gates of Hell. In medieval Europe, most people believed that if you behaved badly while you were alive, your soul would end up somewhere horrible after you died. This place was called Hell, and it was often described as a fiery pit beneath the earth where the wicked were punished. Explorers of the underworld should brace themselves for a bumpy ride...

MAPPING HELL

In his *Inferno*, Dante described Hell as a giant funnel leading toward the center of the Earth. He said it was divided into nine layers, or circles, with the lower layers reserved for the worst sinners. In each circle of Hell, human souls were subjected to different punishments depending on the crimes they had committed while alive. Fortune tellers, whose practice is forbidden in the Bible, had their heads fixed on backward to stop them from seeing what lies ahead. Thieves had their hands tied behind their backs with snakes, while gluttons—those who were greedy for food and drink—wallowed forever in a flood of filth.

- Darkness and clouds
- Winds and storms
- Icy rain
- Pool of molten gold
- Stinking swamp
- Fiery pit
- Sea of boiling blood
- Dark pit of demons
- Lake of ice

Scary Scenes

In medieval times, the walls of Christian churches were often adorned with grisly paintings showing people being boiled in cauldrons, thrown into furnaces, or skewered with pitchforks. These terrifying visions of Hell were intended to frighten people into behaving themselves and obeying the rules of the Church.

For medieval Christians, the most terrifying thing about Hell was that there was no escape: its torments lasted for eternity.

The Devil's Lair

Many people believed that the lord of Hell—the Devil—was the source of all evil. This nightmarish figure had many names: Satan, Beelzebub, Father of Lies. The Devil was the enemy and opposite of God, just as Hell was the opposite of Heaven. Some stories described the Devil as a fallen angel called Lucifer, who had turned against God and been cast down into Hell. Medieval drawings gave the Devil a scary mixture of human and animal features, including horns, a tail, goat's legs, and bat's wings.

The thirteenth-century mathematician Michael Scot came up with the strangely precise calculation that the underworld contained 14,198,580 demons!

THE OTHERWORLD: DREAMLIKE FAIRYLAND FROM CELTIC MYTHS

The Celtic people lived in Britain, Ireland, and western Europe from about 3,000 years ago. According to their myths, if you followed the golden path of the sunset across the ocean to the west, you might eventually find the Otherworld: a beautiful place where gods and fairies lived alongside the spirits of the dead. In the Otherworld it was always summer, the trees bore plentiful fruits and flowers, and the sounds of enchanted music and birdsong drifted on the fragrant breeze. Some stories said that the Otherworld could be reached through caves, burial mounds, or lakes. It was hidden from human eyes by a mist of invisibility, but on certain nights of the year the delicate veil separating the Otherworld from our own was drawn aside...

The Otherworld has many names: Irish stories tell of Tír na nÓg, the Land of Youth, and Mag Mell, the Plain of Honey. In Welsh folklore it is known as Annwn, and in English legends it is linked to Avalon, the Isle of Apples.

Legends say that the Otherworld can be reached through magic portals in these locations.

CKMA
OD
OWEYNAGAT CAVE

AND

NEWGRANGE BURIAL MOUND
LOUGH GUR

THE HOUSE OF DONN

The god of the dead in Irish mythology was Donn. Some believed that when a person died, their soul traveled to Tech Duinn, the House of Donn, which lay on a rocky island off the western coast. From here, the spirits of the dead would travel onward to the Otherworld. Today, the House of Donn is sometimes associated with a tiny island named Bull Rock off the shores of County Cork. This jutting rock is pierced by a natural tunnel, which some say the dead pass through on their journey over the sea, toward the setting sun.

In Irish legends, the warrior Oisín falls in love with the goddess Niamh, and goes to live with her in Tír na nÓg.

THROUGH THE VEIL

On the last night of October, the Celts celebrated the Feast of Samhain, when the curtain between this world and the Otherworld became thinner, and the spirits of the dead could return to walk the earth again. Some people set an empty place at dinner for dead relatives, and put a candle in the window to light a pathway home. At other shadowy times—dawn and dusk—the doorway to the Otherworld might swing open, allowing visitors to sneak through.

THE BAG NOZ: GHOSTLY SHIP OF SOULS

The French region of Brittany is surrounded by the wild Atlantic Ocean on three sides, so the sea has always played an important role in the lives and legends of the Breton people. In medieval Brittany, there was a belief that when somebody died, their soul traveled across the water to the west. The ghostly vessel that carried them was called the Bag Noz: the Night Boat. In the dead of night, so the story goes, the souls of the dead would gather on the beach, waiting patiently for the arrival of the Bag Noz.

LAST JOURNEY

The precise destination of the Bag Noz varied depending on the story. Sometimes, the final resting place of the dead was said to be a group of islands at the edge of the world, from which nobody ever returned. In one legend, related by a sixth-century historian called Procopius, the souls of the dead were ferried to an island called "Brittia," which may have been Britain. On some nights, according to the tales, the heartbreaking cries of the dead could be heard as the boat passed by. The Bag Noz was never clearly visible to the living, but its shadowy outline could be glimpsed, under full sail, with a black flag flying at half-mast. As the Night Boat moved over the ocean, it left not a ripple in the waters behind it.

In the legends of Brittany, the souls of the dead gathered on the shores of Baie des Trépassés (the Bay of the Dead) before beginning their journey west.

In some tales, a fisherman would be called to serve as helmsman on the Bag Noz. At the shore, he would find the boat loaded with spirits, ready to sail to the next world.

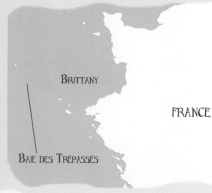

BRITTANY

FRANCE

BAIE DES TRÉPASSÉS

In the Breton language, the phrase "roeñvet en deus war Gornôg" ("he rowed west") is sometimes used to refer to someone's death.

Since ancient times, boats have appeared in afterlife beliefs, carrying the souls of the dead to their final resting place.

SERVANT OF DEATH

In some versions of the story, the Bag Noz was steered by the Ankou, a shadowy servant of death. The Ankou was shown as a skeleton or an old, haggard man, wearing a black robe with a broad-rimmed hat that covered his face, and carrying a large-bladed farming tool called a scythe. But the Ankou did not use his blade to harvest crops: he harvested the souls of the dead. Each parish had a different Ankou, and some believed that the last person to drown each year would become the Ankou for the following year. Only once this soul had served its time was it free to rest.

THE WILD HUNT: PHANTOM RIDERS OF THE NIGHT

If ever you are wandering the lonely moors on a winter's night, and you hear strange howls carried on the cold air, then beware the riders of the Wild Hunt... This noisy troop of phantoms thunders across the pages of European folklore, accompanied by baying hounds, pounding hooves, and trumpeting horns. There are many versions of the Wild Hunt: this riotous rabble is made up of overlapping layers of legend. But most of the tales say that at certain times of year, the dead begin to stir, riding out on flame-eyed horses over moor and heath, field and forest. The ghoulish members of this flying hunting party terrify all who encounter them, and are said to snatch up souls to join their ragged crew.

The Wild Hunt has appeared in stories for centuries, but it first received its name from the German fairytale collector Jacob Grimm in 1835.

BAD OMENS

According to legend, the arrival of the Wild Hunt was an unlucky omen, foretelling death, war, or plague. Merely hearing the barking of the hounds was bad enough, but actually seeing the ghostly riders was even more disastrous: anyone laying eyes on the hunters might be seized up and carried off to join them in the land of the dead.

The ghostly riders were most likely to appear on All Hallows' Eve in October, or during the Germanic festival of Yule at the end of December.

Stories of the Wild Hunt are common across Europe, particularly in the locations shown here.

GREAT BRITAIN

CADER IDRIS

GERMANY

SOLLING FOREST

FRANCE

FONTAINEBLEAU

LEADER OF THE PACK

In Germanic and Norse mythology, the leader of the Wild Hunt was the god Odin, also known as Woden. In Welsh legends it was Gwyn ap Nudd, lord of the dead, who rode a demon horse and commanded a pack of hell-hounds. According to English folklore, the master of this band of shadows was Herne the Hunter: a forest spirit recognizable by his crown of antlers. Sometimes, the leader of the hunt was said to be the Devil himself, gathering up the souls of sinners.

Tales of the Wild Hunt may have been inspired by an ancient fear of the sound of howling wolves, or of natural phenomena such as thunder and lightning.

AFRICA

This huge, diverse continent has given us countless stories of the afterlife, including those of the frightening ancient Egyptian underworld. Some traditional African lands of the dead were thought to lie close to home: in a village just out of reach, down a burrow in the ground, or on the opposite bank of a river. Others were more distant realms that lay far away across the ocean, or among the stars.

ASAMANDO: Ashanti land of the dead

UGHOTON: Historic port from where the dead were once believed to depart in canoes

GHANA

NIGERIA

FARO'S REALM: Some Bambara people believed the water spirit Faro looked after spirits of the dead until they were reborn.

CARRIED BY BEES: In Bambuti beliefs, the soul may be carried to the afterlife by bees

DRC

ATLANTIC OCEAN

ANGOLA

THE KALUNGA LINE Boundary between worlds

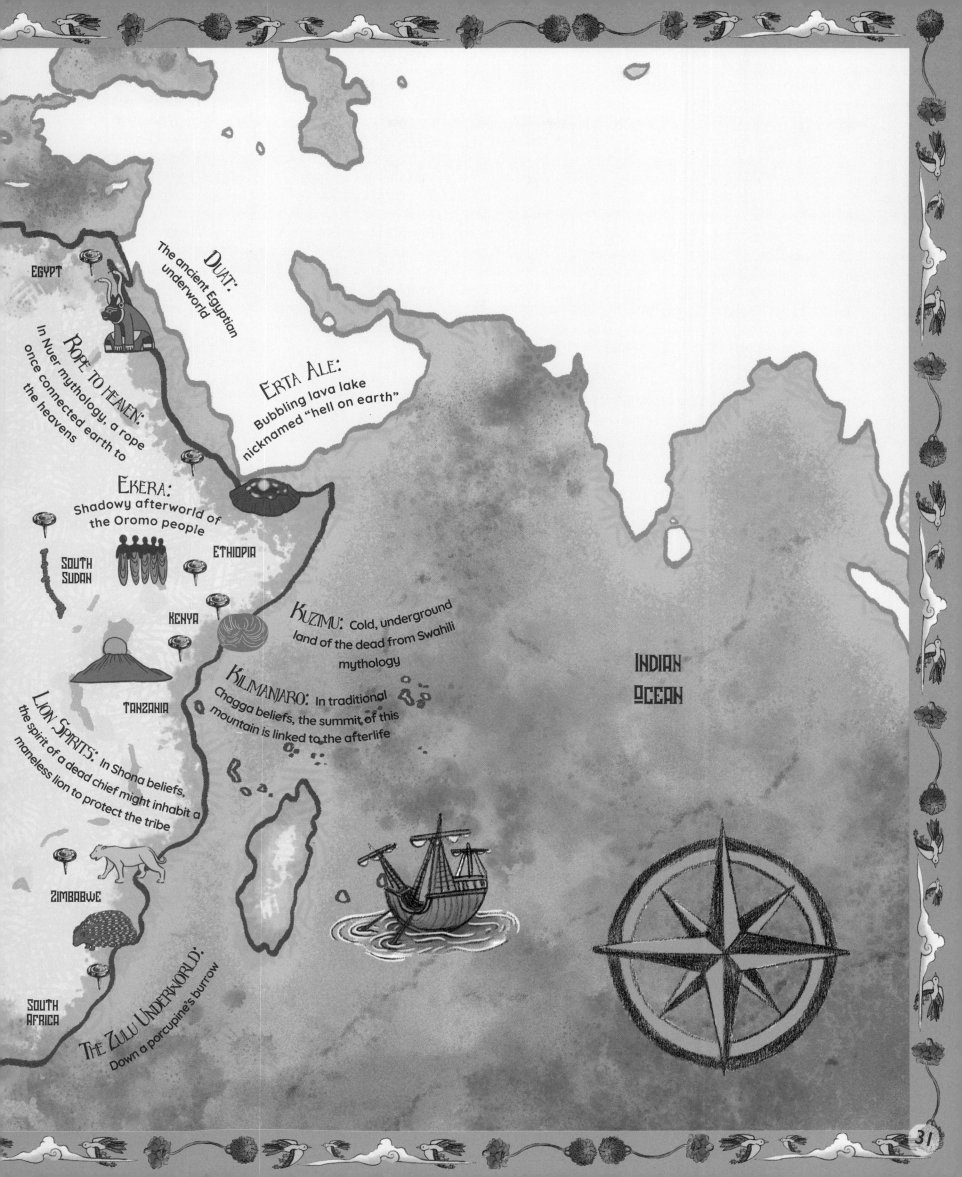

EGYPT

DUAT:
The ancient Egyptian
underworld

ROPE TO HEAVEN:
In Nuer mythology, a rope
once connected earth to
the heavens

ERTA ALE:
Bubbling lava lake
nicknamed "hell on earth"

EKERA:
Shadowy afterworld of
the Oromo people

SOUTH
SUDAN

ETHIOPIA

KENYA

KUZIMU: Cold, underground
land of the dead from Swahili
mythology

KILIMANJARO: In traditional
Chagga beliefs, the summit of this
mountain is linked to the afterlife

INDIAN
OCEAN

TANZANIA

LION SPIRITS: In Shona beliefs,
the spirit of a dead chief might inhabit a
maneless lion to protect the tribe

ZIMBABWE

SOUTH
AFRICA

THE ZULU UNDERWORLD:
Down a porcupine's burrow

DUAT: THE ANCIENT EGYPTIAN UNDERWORLD

The ancient Egyptians spent a great deal of time and effort preparing for the afterlife. Many of the buildings and artifacts we associate with them today—pyramids, mummies, tombs—are related to the idea of life after death. The goal of an ancient Egyptian was to reach the heavenly A'aru, Field of Reeds: a riverside paradise said to lie far away to the east, where the sun rises. To get there, they had to pass a series of tests as they made their way through a terrifying underworld: Duat.

A Perilous Journey

First, the underworld traveler had to pass through twelve gates, guarded by terrifying serpents that breathed fire or venom. At each of these barriers, the dead had to recite the secret name of the dagger-wielding god who watched over the gate. Other hazards included lakes of fire, crocodiles, wild dogs, rivers of boiling water, and baboons that tried to decapitate traveling souls. If they made it past all of these pitfalls, the dead reached the great Hall of Judgment, presided over by Osiris, Lord of the Underworld.

Model boats were often placed in tombs, to provide transport for the afterlife.

The ancient Egyptian civilization grew up on the fertile lands surrounding the River Nile, in northeast Africa.

RIVER NILE

EGYPT

Priests prepared the dead for the afterlife, removing the organs and drying out the body. This is called mummification.

THE BOOK OF THE DEAD

The ancient Egyptians had a guidebook for getting into heaven: the Book of the Dead. This was a series of spells and instructions written in hieroglyphs on papyrus scrolls, to help the dead make it through the underworld. These texts have been discovered in burial chambers dating from about 3,500 years ago. At first, these fast-track tickets to heaven were just for royalty, but as time passed, their use spread to rich and poor alike.

Some believed that there were three parts to a person's soul. The ka stayed with the body, the ba could leave and return to the tomb, while the akh journeyed to the Field of Reeds.

THE WEIGHING OF THE HEART

In the Hall of Judgment, a final test determined if the soul was worthy of heaven. The dog-headed god Anubis took the heart of the traveler and weighed it on the Scales of Justice against a feather. A pure heart was lighter than air. But a heart heavier than the feather, weighed down by jealousy or ingratitude, failed the test and was gobbled up by Ammit, Devourer of the Dead: part-lion, part-hippopotamus, part-crocodile. Only virtuous souls survived this ordeal and were allowed to travel onward to the Field of Reeds.

33

THE KALUNGA LINE: BOUNDARY BETWEEN WORLDS

The kingdom of Kongo, in West-Central Africa, rose to power in the fourteenth century and ruled over a large territory, until its collapse in the early twentieth century. The Kongolese people believed that when somebody died, their spirit followed the path of the setting sun across the ocean toward the west. The distant horizon was thought to be the border between the world of the living and the realm of the dead: it was called the Kalunga Line. According to Kongolese beliefs, a human soul was eternal. Death was not the end, but merely a point on the journey in the circle of life. Spirits that crossed the Kalunga Line might one day return, born again in the world of the living.

People who wanted to communicate with their ancestors would sometimes carve symbols into the shells of sea turtles. They would release the creatures into the ocean to carry the messages across the Kalunga Line.

Some spirits of the dead that had crossed the Kalunga Line were thought to take the form of chalk-white fish called simbi.

CROSSING OVER

Some Kongolese people believed that when spirits crossed the Kalunga Line and arrived in Mpemba, the land of the dead, their skin turned white—the color of death. In the fifteenth century, when light-skinned Portuguese sailors first arrived in West Africa, some people saw them as spirits returned from the afterlife. Between the fifteenth and nineteenth centuries, European slave traders kidnapped millions of African people and transported them across the Atlantic Ocean to colonies in the Americas, where they were forced to work in brutal conditions. To the Kongolese, it seemed that these people had been taken to the land of death. One belief among enslaved Africans in the colonies was that when they died, their spirits would fly back over the ocean, crossing the Kalunga Line to return home.

Across many parts of west Africa, rivers and oceans were seen as boundaries between the earthly world and the world of spirits.

REPUBLIC OF THE CONGO

DEMOCRATIC REPUBLIC OF THE CONGO

KONGO KINGDOM

ANGOLA

Nowadays, the land that used to make up the Kingdom of Kongo is split between Angola, the Republic of the Congo, and the DRC.

THE ZULU UNDERWORLD: UNCAMA'S ADVENTURES IN UNDERLAND

Across the globe, many stories about the afterlife describe a place that mirrors the world of the living. In these far-away lands or underworlds, the souls of the dead are thought to continue their usual daily activities: farming, cooking, feasting, and so on. Such an afterlife appears in a legend from the Zulu people of South Africa: it is the story of Uncama, a farmer who accidentally visited the underworld... and returned home to tell the tale.

Down the Porcupine Hole

Uncama was annoyed. He had grown a fine crop of millet, but every night a porcupine devoured some of his plants. One morning, waking to find the pest had struck again, Uncama decided enough was enough. He took his trusty spear and followed a trail left by the porcupine through the dewy grass. It led to a burrow in the ground. Uncama squeezed into the hole, in hot pursuit of his prickly foe. The tunnel ran deep underground, and as it twisted and turned, Uncama's eyes grew accustomed to the gloom. Eventually, he saw light ahead. He emerged into an underground village, where the air was filled with the sounds of barking dogs and playing children. Uncama had arrived in the underworld.

In a similar tale from Uganda, a hunter follows a rat into a hole that leads to the kingdom of the god of death, Walumbe.

SOUTH AFRICA

KwaZulu-Natal
(traditional territory of the Zulu people)

36

RETURN JOURNEY

Uncama hadn't meant to travel this far, and he was afraid that the villagers would harm him. Without pausing, he retreated the way he had come. When he arrived home, his wife cried out in terror to see him. It had been many days since Uncama disappeared: everyone believed he had died. Indeed, his funeral had already happened. No one was expecting this traveler to return from the underworld.

In some versions of the legend, when Uncama returns home he realizes he has been gone not for several days, but many years.

37

ASAMANDO: ASHANTI LAND OF THE DEAD

Many legends tell us that the realm of the dead is a far-away place from which no one can ever return. But in some stories, a brave traveler visits the afterlife and returns to the world of the living. The Ashanti people of Ghana tell the story of Kwasi Benefo, a farmer who was so heartbroken about the deaths of his wives that he decided to visit them in Asamando, land of the dead.

In Ashanti beliefs, Asamando was an invisible world that lay within reach of the world of the living, from which the voices of the dead could sometimes be heard.

WEST AFRICA

GHANA

THE TALE OF KWASI BENEFO

Kwasi Benefo had many cattle and plentiful fields, but he longed for a wife to share his happiness with. One day, he met a kind woman—they married and were content, until she became ill and died. Kwasi was heartbroken, but eventually his friends convinced him to marry again. However, tragically his second wife died as well. When Kwasi's third wife was killed by a falling tree, he was filled with despair. For several years he lived alone in the wilderness. Then he moved to another village and married a woman there. But when she also died, Kwasi's spirit was crushed, and he returned to his homeland.

One night, he decided to find his way to the land of the dead. He walked until he came to a forest where the dead were buried. He stumbled through the darkness, emerging at the edge of a strange river. Desperate to cross, he waded in, but the waters were too deep, the current too strong. Broken, Kwasi collapsed on the bank.

"What are you doing here?" someone called from the far shore. Kwasi looked up to see an elderly woman on the river bank. "The living cannot enter the land of the dead," she said, gently. Kwasi realized this must be Amokye, who guards the entrance to the other world. "If you won't let me in," he replied, "I will sit here until I die." Seeing his suffering, Amokye calmed the river, allowing Kwasi to cross.

When he reached the village of the dead, he heard laughter and voices, but couldn't see anyone: the dead were invisible. He entered a house and his heart filled with joy to hear familiar voices singing. Kwasi's wives were there! They told him he needed to continue living, and that when the time came for him to die, he would return to them. Kwasi fell into a deep sleep, and woke to find himself back in the forest. He returned to his village, finally at peace with the deaths of his loved ones. He married again, and he and his wife lived to a happy old age.

Ashanti women were sometimes buried in a loincloth called an amoasie, with beads around their waist to give as payment to Amokye, guardian of the land of the dead.

39

PLUTO'S GATE: Ancient temple once believed to be an entrance to the underworld

DARVAZA CRATER: Pit of flaming gas known as the Gate of Hell

MOUNT KUNLUN: Mythical portal to paradise in the Taoist religion

IRKALLA: Mesopotamian underworld

THE CHINVAT BRIDGE: Perilous route to Zoroastrian heaven

THE BUDDHIST UNDERWORLD: Home of Yama, god of death

SHEOL: Underground land of the dead from the Hebrew Bible

JANNAH: Islamic paradise garden

SVARGA: Among the Hindu seven heavens

TURKMENISTAN

TURKEY

ISRAEL

IRAQ

IRAN

NEPAL

SAUDI ARABIA

INDIA

INDIAN OCEAN

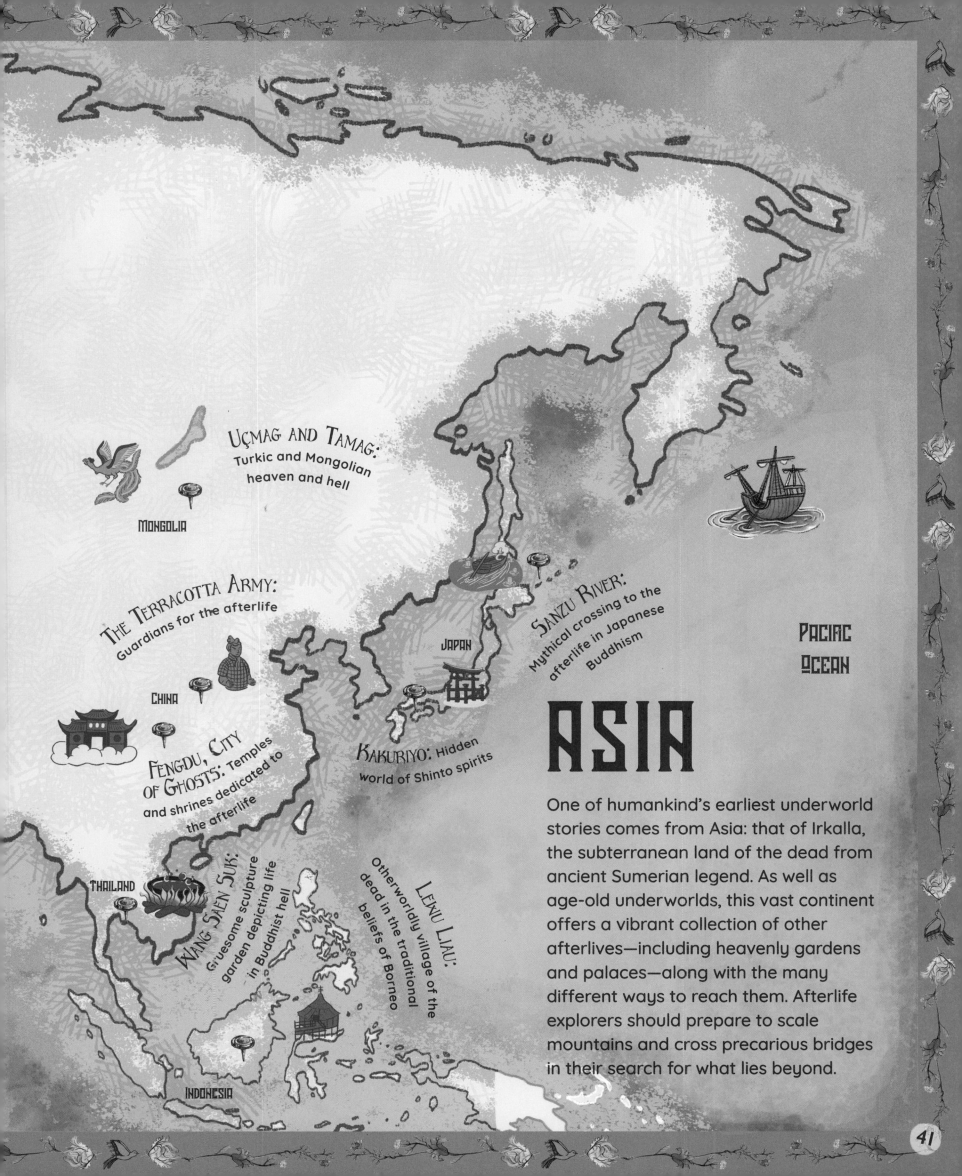

UÇMAG AND TAMAG: Turkic and Mongolian heaven and hell

MONGOLIA

THE TERRACOTTA ARMY: Guardians for the afterlife

CHINA

FENGDU, CITY OF GHOSTS: Temples and shrines dedicated to the afterlife

SANZU RIVER: Mythical crossing to the afterlife in Japanese Buddhism

JAPAN

KAKURIYO: Hidden world of Shinto spirits

PACIFIC OCEAN

THAILAND

WANG SAEN SUK: Gruesome sculpture garden depicting life in Buddhist hell

LEKIU LIAU: Otherworldly village of the dead in the traditional beliefs of Borneo

INDONESIA

ASIA

One of humankind's earliest underworld stories comes from Asia: that of Irkalla, the subterranean land of the dead from ancient Sumerian legend. As well as age-old underworlds, this vast continent offers a vibrant collection of other afterlives—including heavenly gardens and palaces—along with the many different ways to reach them. Afterlife explorers should prepare to scale mountains and cross precarious bridges in their search for what lies beyond.

IRKALLA: THE FIRST UNDERWORLD

To visit the shadowy underworld of Irkalla, we must travel back to the dawn of human history. One of the world's first civilizations was that of the Sumerians, who lived in Mesopotamia about 6,000 years ago. The Sumerians built cities, learned to make pottery and bronze, and invented writing. Pieces of this writing survive to this day, preserved on clay tablets, giving us some of the earliest stories about the afterlife. The Sumerians believed that the land of the dead was located deep below the surface of the earth.

LAND OF NO RETURN

Known by many names—Irkalla, Kur, the Great Below, the Land of No Return—the Sumerian underworld was seen as a dark, desolate city in a vast underground cavern. In this gloomy place, there was no light, no food, and no water. The spirits of the dead had to drink dust and eat clay. Irkalla was fortified by seven locked gates, so that souls could not return to the world of the living. Although it was bleak, it was not a place of punishment for wrongdoings in life: the Sumerians believed that everyone ended up here, and all were treated equally in death.

MESOPOTAMIA

ZAGROS MOUNTAINS

ARABIAN PENINSULA

Mesopotamia lay in western Asia. To the east are the Zagros Mountains, where some people believed a staircase led down to the gates of the underworld.

Irkalla was said to lie beneath an underground ocean called the Abzu.

The underworld was ruled by Ereshkigal, queen of the dead. This powerful goddess was one of the most feared and respected of all the Sumerian gods. She looked after the souls of the dead, ensuring that they never escaped to the world above.

JOURNEY TO THE UNDERWORLD

One of the world's oldest underworld stories is the legend of Inanna's Descent. One day, Inanna, queen of the heavens, decided to seize the underground throne of her sister Ereshkigal. She dressed in her finest robes, put on her crown and breastplate, and took her rod of power. She told her advisor Ninshubur to send help if she hadn't returned in three days.

Inanna reached the first gate of the underworld and knocked sharply. But Ereshkigal was not happy to see her high-and-mighty sister. She insisted that Inanna obey the rules of the underworld, where everyone was equal. As Inanna passed through the seven gates, she was stripped of her finery, until she arrived in her sister's throne room, naked and powerless. Then, Ereshkigal turned Inanna into a corpse and hung her from a hook.

When three days had passed and Inanna hadn't returned, Ninshubur asked the gods for help. Eventually, Ereshkigal agreed to revive and release Inanna, on the condition that someone be sent to the underworld to take her place. Inanna chose her unfaithful husband Dumuzi, because he had not mourned for her while she was gone. And so, Dumuzi was dragged by demons to the underworld, Inanna returned to the world above, and clever Ereshkigal kept her iron grip on her kingdom.

UÇMAG AND TAMAG: ABOVE AND BELOW

In the ancient traditions of the Mongolian and Turkic people from Central Asia, there were many beliefs about the afterlife. Some viewed the world as divided into different layers. In the middle was the human world. Above this, the sky god Ülgen ruled over a kingdom of light among the mountaintops: a heavenly place known as Uçmag. And below the earth was a gloomy underworld ruled by Erlik, the god of death. In this shadowy place, known as Tamag, the spirits of those who had lived wicked lives were punished by demons.

Yayik was a son of the sky god Ülgen. A protector of humankind, Yayik sent a Yayutshi to watch over every person from birth until death.

ERLIK: LORD OF THE UNDERWORLD

The enemy of the sky god was Erlik: bringer of sickness and king of Tamag. In some myths, Erlik was a son of Ülgen, banished to the world below for his pride and ambition (similar to the Devil in Christian stories). Before Erlik left, he snatched as many people as he could and brought them to Tamag to be his servants. It was said that in Tamag, the dead were flung into a cauldron of burning tar. If they had been very bad they would sink to the bottom. However, if they had done some good during their lives they might be rescued by Yayutshis, who would pull them out of the tar by their hair and fly them up to heaven.

KINGDOM OF LIGHT

When a person died, if they had led a good life, their spirit might transform into a bird and soar up to heaven, or be carried aloft by a kind guardian spirit known as a Yayutshi. The powerful sky god Ülgen was believed to live in the highest layer of heaven, above the moon and stars.

Each person was believed to have a guardian angel, called a Yayutshi.

In Turkic mythology, the Konrul was a huge, flame-feathered bird similar to a phoenix.

Kormos were evil spirits that lived in Tamag. They visited the human world to lead people astray and drag them down to the underworld.

Burkhan Khaldun ("God Mountain") is the most sacred mountain in Mongolia today. It is believed that here, spiritual leaders called shamans can communicate with the gods.

BURKHAN KHALDUN

MONGOLIA

45

JANNAH: ISLAMIC PARADISE GARDEN

Islam teaches that there is life after death. For believers who have lived faithfully and done more good deeds than bad, a peaceful afterlife in a heavenly garden is the reward. In the Quran, the holy book of Islam, Jannah—meaning "paradise"—is described as a beautiful garden of shady trees and flowing rivers. For the people of the hot, dry Arabian Peninsula, where Islam was founded in the seventh century, the idea of this lush, cool garden would have been delightfully enticing.

Paradise is said to be so beautiful that it is difficult to describe, or even imagine. This illustration depicts an earthly Islamic garden, which mirrors certain elements of the paradise described in the Quran.

DAY OF JUDGMENT

In Islam, everyone is said to have two angels, one on each shoulder, who write down their good and bad deeds during their lives. It is believed that the dead will remain in their graves until Yawm ad-din: the Day of Judgment. When this day comes, they will be judged by Allah, the one god, according to their book of deeds. If there are more good deeds than bad, angels will lead them into paradise, where they will live forever. However, if their bad deeds outnumber their good, they might end up in the fiery pit of Jahannam (hell). According to Islam, Allah is a kind and merciful judge—if someone is truly sorry for their bad deeds, they will be forgiven and can still reach paradise.

The city of Mecca in Saudi Arabia is the holiest city in Islam, as it was the birthplace of the Prophet Muhammad.

MECCA

ARABIAN PENINSULA

GARDEN OF DELIGHTS

The garden of Jannah overflows with the scents of fragrant flowers and luscious fruits, while the gentle sounds of burbling rivers and sweetly singing birds drift on the air. The sight of majestic palaces and pavilions provide a feast for the eyes, while warm sunlight and refreshing breezes dance over the skin. In Jannah, everyone lives in perfect peace and happiness.

There are four rivers in paradise, running with water, milk, honey, and wine.

SVARGA: AMONG THE SEVEN HEAVENS

According to Hinduism, the heavenly realm of Svarga exists among the clouds that surround the lofty peaks of the sacred Mount Meru. Unlike the Christian and Muslim ideas of paradise, heaven for Hindu believers is not a final destination, but a stopping-off point on the great journey of life, death, and rebirth.

Indra is the Hindu god of the sky, who dispenses rain, thunder, and lightning.

The queen of Svarga is the powerful goddess Shachi, wife of Indra.

The Hindu World

Ancient Hindu writings describe the world as divided into 14 different layers, or lokas: there are seven lower realms and seven upper realms. At the center of everything is a mythical, golden mountain, Mount Meru, said to be 84,000 yojanas high (which is more than half a million miles—85 times the diameter of Earth)! Above the cloud-covered pinnacles of Mount Meru are the various heavens, which are home to different gods and goddesses.

The Cycle of Life

The belief in reincarnation is important in Hinduism. The idea is that when you die, your soul—or atman—is born again in a different living thing, which could be a human, an animal, or a plant. This cycle of death and rebirth is called samsara. Between your different lives, your soul might rest for a while in one of the heavens, before returning to the earth. After you have lived many lives and gained wisdom, you may be able to break free from the cycle, achieving the state of moksha. At this time, your soul will join with the Supreme Being, called Brahman, just as a small river merges into the great ocean.

In Svarga lies the glimmering city of Amaravati, home of the god Indra. He dwells in a vast, bejeweled palace surrounded by beautiful gardens.

A many-trunked white elephant named Airavata guards the entrance to the celestial city. This formidable beast is sometimes ridden by Indra.

The Law of Karma

In the cycle of life, karma is important. Karma is the force created by your actions—whether they are good or bad. If your actions in one life result in good karma, then the next life will be easier; if your actions create bad karma, the next life will be a struggle. If you have good karma, you might spend a while enjoying the delights of the heavenly Svarga before you begin your next life.

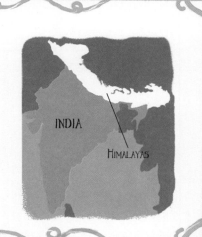

It is said that the Himalayan Mountains are the foothills of the sacred Mount Meru, which lies at the center of the universe.

INDIA

HIMALAYAS

THE BUDDHIST UNDERWORLD: HOME OF YAMA, GOD OF DEATH

Buddhism began in northern India about 2,500 years ago. Like Hindus, Buddhists believe in reincarnation: that when someone dies, they will be born again in a new body. Doing bad things in one life creates bad karma, so you might be reborn in a frightening place: the underworld. Unlike other afterlives that last for eternity, this is a place of only temporary punishment—although it still might last for billions of years! Ancient Buddhist writings say that beneath the ordinary world, stacked on top of each other, are many cavernous layers of the underworld, each containing a different hell, or Naraka. In Northern Buddhism there are said to be eight cold hells and eight hot hells.

The Citipati are a pair of dancing skeletons from Northern Buddhism. They remind people that life is temporary.

THE REALMS OF REBIRTH

Buddhists believe that the type of karma you create as you move through your life affects how you will be reborn in the next life. There are six possible realms of rebirth:

The heavenly **Realm of the Gods** is the most pleasant of the six realms, but a stay here is only temporary.

The **Realm of the Demi-Gods** is populated by jealous beings who fight among themselves and make war on the gods.

In the **Realm of the Humans** it is possible to achieve enlightenment (nirvana) and break free from the whole cycle.

Those in the **Realm of the Animals** cannot attain wisdom, because animals are driven by competition and their basic needs.

The **Realm of the Hungry Ghosts** is home to invisible, restless spirits that live in a state of constant craving.

Being reborn into the **Realm of Hell** is the result of a lifetime of greed and hatred.

In the "cold" hells, there are many horrible tortures relating to the freezing conditions.

LORD OF DEATH

In Buddhism and Hinduism, Yama is the god of death and the underworld. With his angry, bull-like face, flaming horns, and crown of skulls, Yama appears terrifying. But he is not seen as an evil figure. Instead, his job is to remind people that life won't last forever, and that they should act kindly in their thoughts, words, and deeds.

In the "hot" hells, punishments include being chopped up by demons, squished by rocks, torn apart by ravenous animals, and of course, tortured with fire.

Buddhists follow the teachings of the Buddha, the "enlightened one." His name was Siddhartha Gautama, and he was born in Lumbini, Nepal, around 2,500 years ago.

NEPAL — LUMBINI

INDIA

51

THE TERRACOTTA ARMY: GUARDIANS FOR THE AFTERLIFE

On March 29, 1974, a group of Chinese farmers were digging a well when they came across something strange. Several feet down, buried in the red sandy soil, they discovered pieces of a life-sized soldier made from baked clay. A team of archaeologists were sent to investigate, and were staggered by what they found. They unearthed soldier after soldier, arranged in rows: a vast army of statues more than 2,000 years old, buried underground to protect the tomb of their master—the first emperor of China—for all eternity. This discovery was one of the most astonishing finds of the twentieth century—and it tells us a lot about the ancient Chinese view of the afterlife.

The Quest for Eternal Life

Qin Shi Huang was China's first emperor. During his reign, which took place roughly 2,250 years ago, he united several warring kingdoms into one nation. Some stories say that the emperor was obsessed with living forever, and sent his servants to the farthest edges of the kingdom to search for the elixir of life: a potion that would make him immortal. Despite these efforts, the search was fruitless, and the emperor died at the age of 49. However, if he couldn't live forever, he at least wanted to be well prepared for the afterlife, which is why he commanded the building of an enormous necropolis—a city of the dead—to house his tomb, complete with everything he would need for the next life.

The Terracotta Army is the world's largest group of life-sized statues, but they were never meant to be seen by the living: they were designed for the world of the dead.

The ancient Chinese historian Sima Qian wrote that after the necropolis was finished, some workers were buried alive inside, so they would never reveal the secrets of the emperor's tomb.

PREPARING FOR THE AFTERLIFE

Ancient China had a rich and varied culture, so there were many different views of the afterlife in different regions and at different times. One important belief was that death was not the end, but a continuation of the earthly life. When someone died, they were buried with all the objects they would need in the next chapter. The necropolis of Qin Shi Huang was an extreme example of this, complete not just with an army of soldiers to protect the emperor, but also terracotta acrobats, musicians, and strongmen to keep him entertained.

The terracotta warriors were discovered about 25 miles northeast of the city of Xi'an.

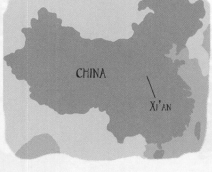

CHINA

XI'AN

Most of the warriors measure about 70 inches. The largest stand over 6 feet tall.

ANCIENT WONDER

According to ancient reports, it took some 700,000 workers nearly 40 years to build the emperor's tomb and his clay bodyguards. In total, there are thought to be up to 670 terracotta horses, 130 battle chariots, and 8,000 soldiers, although only about 2,000 of these have been unearthed. These endless rows of warrior guardians were created with painstaking detail: they have different faces, hairstyles, and expressions, so no two look exactly the same. The figures had different roles in the ghostly army: many were armored foot-soldiers, but there were also archers, charioteers, horsemen, officers, and generals.

THE CHINVAT BRIDGE: PERILOUS ROUTE TO HEAVEN

One of the world's oldest religions, Zoroastrianism, began about 3,500 years ago in Persia (modern-day Iran). According to traditional beliefs, three days after a person dies, their soul begins its journey to a heavenly place called the House of Song. However, to reach it, every soul must first cross the daunting Chinvat Bridge, which separates the world of the living from the world of the dead. One false step, and the soul might plummet into the cold, dark abyss below.

The bridge is guarded by two celestial dogs that bark to chase away the demons that snap at the heels of traveling souls.

THE FINAL JUDGMENT

In traditional Zoroastrian beliefs, how a person behaves in life affects what happens to them after they die. Before crossing the Chinvat Bridge, a soul is brought before the angel Rashnu, who acts as a judge. Then, the soul comes face to face with its daena: a figure that represents the conscience. If someone has lived a good life, a fragrant breeze will blow, and their daena will take the form of a beautiful young woman who guides them across the bridge, which widens as they walk until it is the width of nine spears laid end to end.

However, if a person's wicked actions outweigh the good, a putrid wind will blow, their daena will appear as a frightening hag, and the bridge will shrink until it is as narrow and sharp as the blade of a sword. No wicked souls can make it across; instead, they topple into the void, to be dragged by terrifying creatures to the House of Lies.

THE HOUSE OF LIES

Beneath the Chinvat Bridge is a hellish place known as the House of Lies. In this dark, crowded, stinking underworld, the souls of the wicked are tormented by snakes, scorpions, and demons. There is, however, a glimmer of hope, because these tortures won't last forever. One day, so the ancient writings say, there will be a mighty battle in which the creator god, Ahura Mazda, will defeat the forces of evil and bring all the dead back to life, to live together in a paradise on earth.

As departing souls cross the bridge, they are protected by the angel Sorush, who fights off prowling demons.

In the House of Song, the souls of the virtuous will meet the supreme god Ahura Mazda.

Asto Vidatu, the "Dissolver of Bones," is a demon of death who tries to catch the souls of the dead as they cross the bridge.

The earthly end of the Chinvat Bridge was said to stand on a mythical mountain known as Harburz, or High Hara. This legendary peak has been linked with the Alborz Mountains of northern Iran.

The idea of a bridge to heaven occurs in many different religions. In Islam, the way to paradise lies across the razor-thin bridge of As-Sirat, under which the fires of hell burn.

ALBORZ MOUNTAINS

IRAN

KAKURIYO: HIDDEN WORLD OF SPIRITS

Shinto is Japan's oldest religion, dating back more than 2,000 years. For the ancient Japanese, there was no single, fixed view of the afterlife: there were several different realms of the dead. Some said the spirits of those who had died traveled to Ne-no-kuni, the Land of Roots: a place across the ocean where souls are born. Some went to Yomi, a dark underworld, while others journeyed to the peak of a sacred mountain. Many believed that the souls of the dead didn't travel far, but instead passed to Kakuriyo: a hidden world within our own.

THE INVISIBLE WORLD

For many people, death was not seen as the end, but a time of change. When someone died, they withdrew from Utsushiyo, the visible world of the living, and crossed the border into another realm: the invisible world of Kakuriyo. Kakuriyo was not to be found beneath the earth, high in the clouds, or on a far-off island: instead, this hidden world lay alongside our own, overlapping the visible world. It was said that the spirits of the dead dwelt near burial sites or Shinto shrines, watching over, guiding, and protecting their friends and relatives in the world of the living.

JAPAN

ITSUKUSHIMA SHRINE

A torii is a special gateway at the entrance to a Shinto shrine, which marks a shift between the everyday world and the sacred world. The famous "floating" torii of Itsukushima Shrine can be found on the island of Miyajima in Hiroshima Bay.

When somebody dies and passes to the invisible world, many believe that their soul will be greeted by the spirits of their ancestors.

Shinto teachings say that spirits in Kakuriyo can easily see the world of the living, but the living cannot see those in the hidden realm.

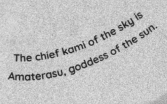

The chief kami of the sky is Amaterasu, goddess of the sun.

HONORING THE KAMI

There is no single all-powerful god in Shinto. Instead, there is a belief in kami: sacred spirits that exist in everything from trees, mountains, and rivers to birds and animals. In Japan there are many Shinto shrines where kami are prayed to and respected—in return, it is believed they will keep away evil spirits and bring health, happiness, and prosperity. Some think that when a person dies, their soul becomes one of the kami, living on in the invisible spirit world.

ARCTIC
OCEAN

SPIRIT HOUSES:
Small graveside houses in Eklutna, thought to provide shelter for the spirits of the dead

ADLIVUN: Watery underworld of the Inuit people

CANADA

GHOST LAND: Village of the dead from the tales of the Tlingit people

BIG SAND: Afterworld of the Gros Ventre people

THE SPIRIT ROAD: Underground trail to the afterlife in the myths of the Thompson River people

PACIFIC
OCEAN

GHOST TOWN: The trickster Bluejay visits this land of the dead to find his sister in a Chinook story

TRAIL OF SPIRITS: Lakota skyway through the stars

USA

KOTHLUWALAWA: Zuni dance-hall of the dead

MEXICO

NORTH AMERICA

Among the numerous tribes and nations of Indigenous American people, there are many different traditional beliefs about life after death. Some groups believe that the dead live on among the stars; others envision nearby spirit worlds, caverns beneath the earth, or heavens on distant mountaintops. To the south, people in modern-day Mexico celebrate the colorful Day of the Dead festival, which has its roots in historic Aztec beliefs about the afterlife.

MICTLAN: The Aztec Underworld

SNAKE BRIDGE:
Crossing to paradise
from Ojibwe legends

GRANDMOTHER
GUARDIAN: Travelers
might meet this figure on
the way to the Winnebago
afterlife

CAUTANTOWWIT'S
HOUSE: Traditional realm
of the dead for the
Algonquian people

GHOST COUNTRY:
The Sun's daughter ends up
here in a Cherokee legend

THE GATES OF GUINEE:
Portal to the Voudou
underworld

DAY OF THE DEAD: Some
believe the dead return to earth
for a short time during this
colorful Mexican festival

ATLANTIC
OCEAN

THE TRAIL OF SPIRITS: SKYWAY THROUGH THE STARS

The Lakota are a group of Indigenous American nations from the Great Plains region. For centuries, Lakota astronomers studied the stars, naming constellations and observing comets, meteor showers, and eclipses. By paying attention to the skies, they could work out the best times to travel, hunt, plant, and harvest. But in the stars, some ancient Lakota people also found an answer to the age-old question of what happens after we die...

Our planet lies on one of the spiraling arms of the Milky Way. From Earth, this vast galaxy appears as a river of light in the sky.

THE GHOST ROAD

The Lakota are a large, diverse group with a long and varied history, so they have many different beliefs about the afterlife. According to some traditions, when a baby is born, they receive a spirit—a wanagi—from the stars. When they die, this same spirit returns to the stars along a pathway in the sky, the Milky Way, known as Wanagi Tacanku, the Ghost Road, or the Trail of Spirits. Some believe that when the wanagi leaves a person's body, it travels to the cup of the Big Dipper constellation, from where it is carried, as if on a stretcher, along the twinkling path of the Milky Way.

Various cultures around the world—including in Central America, South America, and Australia—have seen the Milky Way as a path to the afterlife.

GUARDIAN GODDESS

As a soul travels along the Trail of Spirits, it might come to a fork in the road guarded by an elderly woman known as Hihankara, the Owl Maker. She looks for certain tattoos on the wrist of each spirit, which act like a passport. If travelers cannot show her the correct markings, she casts them back to earth to wander forever as ghosts.

In some Lakota communities, people are buried with beaded moccasins (deerskin shoes) to help their departing spirit as it walks along the Ghost Road.

Many Indigenous American groups share similar beliefs. The Cheyenne call the Milky Way "the Road of the Departed," while in Seminole stories it leads to the City of the West—the final destination for the spirits of the dead.

LIGHTS IN THE SKY

Some say that the Ghost Road leads to Wanagi Makoce, the spirit world, home of departed souls. A place of peace and plenty, here there is no war, sickness, or death—instead there are shady trees, lush grasses, cool waters to drink, and enough food for everyone. In this spirit world, people come together to feast and dance, producing glowing lights in the sky that their relations down on earth can see. We call them the Northern Lights.

Before the arrival of Europeans in North America, the lands of the Lakota people extended across a large area.

MONTANA
NORTH DAKOTA
LAKOTA LANDS
SOUTH DAKOTA
WYOMING
NEBRASKA

KOTHLUWALAWA: DANCE-HALL OF THE DEAD

The Zuni people are Indigenous Americans who have lived among the rugged, majestic, red-rocky landscapes of New Mexico for thousands of years. According to their traditional beliefs, the spirits of the dead travel to a heavenly place that lies beneath the waters of a sacred lake on the Zuni River. When they reach this otherworld—called Kothluwalawa—they are united with the spirits of their ancestors.

In Zuni beliefs, the bringers of clouds and rain are the koko: the spirits of the ancestors.

Since ancient times, the Zuni people have lived along the Zuni River. Their homeland is called Halona Idiwan'a, which means "Middle Place of the World."

HISTORIC ZUNI LANDS

NEW MEXICO

ARIZONA

During special ceremonies, when the Zuni people dance together, they shake the earth so the koko can feel it, even in far-away Kothluwalawa.

JOURNEY TO THE AFTERLIFE

Different Zuni groups have their own particular beliefs about what happens after death, but it is often said that the journey to Kothluwalawa takes four days. Immediately after somebody dies, their family might put food into the fire to send along with the spirit to the afterlife. A person's possessions might be buried with them, or burned and their ashes cast into the Zuni River to be carried to the Great Village at the bottom of the Lake of the Dead.

KOKO: SPIRITS OF THE ANCESTORS

Along with some other Indigenous American groups from the southwest U.S., the Zuni have a belief in the koko, also called kachinas: a group of spirit beings. At the beginning of time, it is said that the Zuni people climbed out of the underworld and crossed a river. Some of the children fell into the water and became frogs, which swam to Kothluwalawa. They were lost to the world of the living, but they turned into koko and danced happily beneath the waters of the lake. When the spirits of the dead reach the afterworld, they also become koko. Sometimes, the koko take the form of clouds and travel back to the world of the living, bringing with them the precious blessing of rain to nourish the earth.

ADLIVUN: WATERY UNDERWORLD OF THE INUIT PEOPLE

Far to the north, in the freezing lands that stretch from Arctic Canada to Greenland, live the Inuit people. For generations, the Inuit have honored the goddess of the ocean: a mighty sea spirit named Sedna. Sedna has power over the winds and waves, and is the mother of the wild creatures of the Arctic waters. According to Inuit beliefs, the spirits of the dead descend to Sedna's underwater kingdom, which is called Adlivun, meaning "those who live beneath us."

SEDNA: QUEEN OF THE OCEAN

In one version of the story, Sedna started out as a wild and unmanageable child with an insatiable appetite. One stormy night, she was so hungry that she tried to eat her parents as they slept. Her father Anguta awoke in horror and bundled her into a canoe, rowing her far out to sea, where he flung her overboard. But Sedna, terrified, clung to the edge of the little boat in desperation. To force her to let go, her father cut off her fingers one by one, until Sedna disappeared beneath the raging waves. As she sank, her fingers transformed into whales, seals, and fish, which gathered around her, and as she reached the sea bed, she felt her body become one with the waters. She was no longer Sedna, the angry young girl. She was Sedna, goddess of the underwater world.

GATHERER OF THE DEAD

The story goes that Sedna conjured a huge wave to punish her father for abandoning her, dragging him down to the underworld, where he lives to this day. His job is to gather up the spirits of the dead, leading them to Adlivun, the land beneath the waves, where they will remain for a year until their souls are at peace. Then, at last, they will make their final journey to Quidlivun, Land of the Moon—a happy place of eternal rest.

It is said that the house of Sedna, made from whale ribs, lies across an icy abyss only passable via a bridge the width of a knife blade.

The Inuit people live across the Arctic region in Alaska, Canada, and Greenland.

ALASKA, USA

ARCTIC OCEAN

CANADA

GREENLAND

Some believe that Sedna, queen of the ocean underworld, will become angry if the creatures of the sea are not properly respected.

JOURNEY TO THE UNDERWORLD

In traditional Inuit beliefs, it is important to keep Sedna happy, because she has the power to lock away sea creatures beneath the ice, where they cannot be caught and eaten. If Sedna is angry, there is a danger that people will starve. However, her rage may be calmed by a visit from a shaman—a wise person whose soul can travel between the human and spirit worlds. In a special ceremony, a shaman's spirit might journey to the underworld to soothe Sedna and comb her unruly hair, until she agrees to release the animals so the hunters can feed their families.

Among different Inuit groups there are many names for Sedna, such as Sassuma Arnaa, which means "mother of the deep" and Takannaaluk, meaning "the one down there."

THE GATES OF GUINEE: PORTAL TO THE VOUDOU UNDERWORLD

The Voudou religion began many centuries ago, in the West African kingdom of Dahomey (now Benin). When enslaved African people were brought to the Caribbean country of Haiti in the 1600s, African traditions blended with Christianity to create new beliefs. In the early 1800s, thousands of Haitian people came to the U.S. state of Louisiana, bringing with them the beliefs of Haitian Voudou. Today, some say that the Gates of Guinee—entrance to the Voudou underworld—can be found in the historic cemeteries of New Orleans!

NEW ORLEANS

USA

Legend has it that the Gates of Guinee can be found somewhere in New Orleans's French Quarter, perhaps in the Saint Louis Cemetery, near the tomb of a famous Voudou priestess named Marie Laveau.

THE VOUDOU AFTERLIFE

There's no fixed set of Voudou beliefs—instead, the teachings are passed down by word of mouth, changing through time. In Haitian Voudou, humans are made up of three parts: the body, the personality (tibonanj), and the immortal spirit (gwobonanj). When someone dies, a ritual is performed to help the spirit leave the body and travel to the land of the dead, known as Guinee: a mysterious place said to lie underwater or below the earth. The spirit remains in Guinee for a year and a day, after which time another ritual is performed to summon it back, so that its living relatives can call on it for guidance and protection. Once a spirit returns from Guinee it might be reborn in a new person, carrying on the cycle of life.

Some believers in Voudou say that people can be brought back from the dead by magic. When this happens, they are called "zombis."

Baron Samedi, also known as Baron Cimetière, is the guardian of cemeteries, protecting the graves of the dead.

When the Baron ventures out of the underworld, he sometimes wears dark glasses to protect his eyes from the light.

BARON SAMEDI

Lingering at the crossroads between life and death is the skeletal figure of Baron Samedi, Voudou father of the dead. Recognizable by his top hat, tailcoat, and skull-topped cane, he welcomes the dead to the afterlife, and protects the living from dying too soon. Although he looks frightening, the Baron is a trickster who likes to laugh, and who teases those who take themselves too seriously. In New Orleans, locals say that there are seven gates to the Voudou underworld, each guarded by a different loa, or spirit. Baron Samedi stands guard over the seventh and final gate.

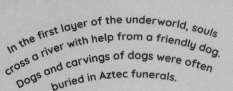

In the first layer of the underworld, souls cross a river with help from a friendly dog. Dogs and carvings of dogs were often buried in Aztec funerals.

In the second layer the traveler, now stripped of clothes, must pass between two huge, clashing mountains.

Next, the dead pick their way down a treacherous slope bristling with razor-sharp stones.

In the fourth layer, souls must cross eight snow-shrouded mountains.

The fifth layer is a dark moorland where the winds are so strong they fling travelers around around like fluttering flags.

Eventful Journey

It was said that before a soul reached its final destination, it embarked on a four-year journey through the levels of the underworld. The voyage was fraught with danger, with new hazards to face in each layer. At last, the soul would be welcomed into Mictlan, the windowless house of the dead. This lowest level of the underworld was a dark, mysterious place, but it was not seen as a place of torture or punishment.

MICTLAN: THE AZTEC UNDERWORLD

In the fifteenth century, the Mexica, or Aztec, people built an empire in what is now central Mexico. They believed that the gods lived in 13 heavens above the human world, while below lay a shadowy underworld with nine different layers. For the Aztecs, what happened after death was decided by the way you died. Warriors slain in battle or people who had been sacrificed to the gods lived on in the eastern land of the Sun for four years, then returned to earth as beautiful hummingbirds. Women who had died in childbirth were destined for a heaven in the west, while people who had drowned went to a flower-filled paradise called Tlalocan, home of the rain god. Most others descended through the underworld until they reached the lowest layer: the realm of Mictlan.

MEXICO   AZTEC EMPIRE

RULERS OF THE DEAD

The lord of Mictlan was the god Mictlantecuhtli. This skeletal figure sat on a throne surrounded by owls, spiders, and the bones of humans, piled up like a grim hoard of treasure. His wife, the queen of the dead, was the goddess Mictecacihuatl. Ancient rituals dedicated to her may be the root of the Day of the Dead festival, celebrated in modern-day Mexican communities each November.

Souls of the dead will not make it through the sixth layer without being pierced by flying arrows.

In the seventh layer, fierce monsters eat the hearts of the dead.

Finally, the soul will arrive in Mictlan, to be greeted by the Lord and Lady of Death.

In the eighth layer, the dead must swim through a deep, black lake, making sure to avoid the serpent that lurks there.

MEXICO

MOUNT RORAIMA: Table-top mountain where the ancestor spirits of the Pemon people are said to dwell

XIBALBA: The Maya Underworld

BELIZE

GUATEMALA

NICARAGUA

GUYANA

MASAYA VOLCANO: This smoke-spewing crater was called the "Mouth of Hell" by Spanish conquistadores

HEDU: The Yanomami heaven

MOCHE PYRAMIDS: Treasures from the tombs of the ancient Moche people show they were buried with items they would need for the afterlife

VILLAGE OF THE DEAD: In Kalapalo beliefs, the dead sing and dance in a village in the sky

THREE PACHAS: The worlds of the Incas

PERU

PACIAC OCEAN

CHILE

DOCK OF SOULS: This curved boardwalk is where wandering souls are said to wait for a boat to the afterlife

EL CALEUCHE: Enchanted ship of the dead

BRAZIL

PROCESSION OF SOULS: The city of Mariana holds an annual parade of white-robed people representing the spirits of the dead

ATLANTIC OCEAN

CENTRAL & SOUTH AMERICA

The ancient Maya people had a detailed—and rather disturbing—vision of the underworld, so afterlife explorers should brace themselves for a perilous journey, beset with demons and dangers. Aside from the hair-raising Maya underworld, the cultures of Central and South America offer many more alluring options, from the mysterious ghost ship of Chilean folklore to the heavenly House of Souls in the beliefs of Brazil's Yanomami people.

XIBALBA:
THE MAYA UNDERWORLD

Underworld explorers beware: the Maya nether-realm was a frightening place! The ancient Maya people lived in southeast Mexico, Guatemala, and Belize more than 1,000 years ago. Like the Aztecs who came after them, the Maya believed in 13 heavens above the earth and a cavernous underworld below. In their myths, these realms were connected by the branches and roots of a mighty world tree. The name of the underworld was Xibalba (pronounced "Shee-bal-ba"), which means "place of fear," and it's not hard to see why...

TWELVE ANGRY GODS

When a person died in the ancient Maya world, they were often buried under the floor of their house, from where it was believed their soul would descend to the underworld. Alongside them were sometimes placed weapons and tools to help them on their perilous journey. To reach Xibalba, the dead first had to travel through a vast underground labyrinth, crisscrossed by rivers of blood, pus, and scorpions. At last, they would reach a grand court ruled over by the lords of the underworld. These were 12 gods of death: terrifying demons with names like Pus Master, Blood Gatherer, and Flying Scab! These Lords of Xibalba sent the dead to six Houses of Endurance, where the poor souls had to contend with fierce jaguars, flying daggers, blood-sucking bats, ice storms, and raging fires.

THE DARK HOUSE

LIFE AFTER DEATH

Some Maya people believed that if a soul could survive the various challenges of Xibalba, it would be reborn from the underworld into a heavenly afterlife. Fortunate souls would rise up from the lower realms, following the pathway of the sun as it ascended into the heavens. In ancient carvings from the Maya city of Palenque, the dead return to life as fruit trees in an eternal orchard.

THE RATTLING HOUSE

THE HOUSE OF JAGUARS

Deadly Game

The *Popol Vuh*, an ancient Maya text, tells the story of the Hero Twins, who were summoned to Xibalba by the gods of death. After making their way past all the traps, the brothers were forced to play a deadly ball game called pok-a-tok, using a ball studded with razor-sharp blades. This game (without the blades) was played in the earthly world too, on large stone courts in Maya cities. Historians believe the rules may have involved keeping the ball in the air using only the knees, hips, elbows, and wrists... and the losing team, or its leader, might have been sacrificed to the gods!

The Hot House

The House of Razor Blades

The House of Bats

The ancient Maya people lived on the Yucatán Peninsula. The landscape is riddled with freshwater sinkholes called cenotes, linked by a branching network of underground rivers. These cenotes were sacred places, seen as portals to the underworld.

YUCATÁN PENINSULA

MEXICO

BELIZE

GUATEMALA HONDURAS

EL CALEUCHE: ENCHANTED SHIP OF THE DEAD

On the mist-shrouded island of Chiloé, which lies off the coast of southern Chile, local people whisper tales of the *Caleuche*: a ghostly galleon whose crew is made up of the souls of drowned sailors. On foggy nights, so the stories say, this mysterious ship may appear, brightly lit with blazing lanterns. From its decks come captivating melodies—snatches of beautiful music that drift across the waters. And sometimes, as the ship passes by, the laughter of its phantom crew can be heard as these lost mariners enjoy an everlasting party.

It's possible that ghost ships are illusions caused by glowing sea creatures, or rays of light bending as they pass through the air.

Sightings of the *Caleuche* were often reported on the island of Chiloé until the middle of the twentieth century.

RESCUED BY MERMAIDS

According to the folklore of Chiloé, two mermaid sisters named La Pincoya and La Sirena Chilota rescue the victims of shipwrecks from the waters. If a drowning sailor is still alive, they will bring him safely back to shore. However, if he has already died, they will carry him to join the crew of the *Caleuche*, where he will spend a happy afterlife among this merry company of spooky seafarers.

74

According to legend, the *Caleuche* could travel underwater, glowing gently from beneath the waves like a submerged moon.

This ghostly ship was said to appear and disappear mysteriously. It could sail head-on into the wind, and pass through other vessels as if by magic.

GHOSTLY CREW

There are many legends about the *Caleuche*. Some say that the ship's crew knows every language, including those of the sea creatures and the birds. These mysterious mariners can transform themselves into seals, dolphins, or other ocean animals. For this reason, the people of the island show great respect to all sea creatures, for any could be a ghostly sailor in disguise. One night a year, the crew of the *Caleuche* are granted shore leave, and return home to comfort their grieving families. Then, they board the ship of souls again as it continues its eternal voyage across the dark waters.

CHILE

CHILOÉ ISLAND

HEDU: THE YANOMAMI HEAVEN

The Yanomami people of the Amazon rainforest have many myths that have been passed down through the generations. According to their traditional beliefs, the world is made up of four flat discs stacked on top of one another like huge plates. At the top is the empty upper sky, next is the lower sky (called Hedu), below that is the earth, and then the underworld. A long time ago, so the legends say, the sky collapsed, smothering the previous earth and squashing it down into the underworld. The earth that people live on today is what remains of the previous sky, which is why the Yanomami people call the forest the "old sky."

UPPER SKY

Our sky, with its sun, moon, and stars, is the underside of Hedu.

The spirits of the dead dwell on the "sky's back" in a House of Souls.

On the earth, Yanomami shamans call upon spirits known as Xapiri to hold up the sky.

SACRED CEREMONY

Some Yanomami people believe that a person's soul resides in their bones. After death, the bones are cremated to release the soul, which travels with the smoke toward the sky. The ashes are kept in a special pot for several months. Then, a ceremony takes place in which the ashes are mixed into soup and drunk by the family of the deceased. This ritual is thought to help the soul travel safely to the "sky's back"—the afterlife.

VENEZUELA

YANOMAMI

BRAZIL

The chaos spirit Xiwãripo and the night spirit Titiri are said to reside in the underworld.

INTO THE SKY

The spirits of the dead are said to travel to the "sky's back": the far side of Hedu. Here, they join their ancestors in the great, circular house (shapono) of the god of thunder. When thunder rumbles, it is sometimes believed that spirits are welcoming a new soul into the sky. The forest surrounding the village of the dead is filled with fruit trees and animals, so the dead never go hungry. In Hedu, there is no pain or sickness, only joyful feasting in the company of long-lost friends and relations. Some believe that eventually, the souls die a second time, transform into vultures, and soar even higher to the upper sky.

HEDU

In the lowest layer live the Aõpatari: an ancient people who were pushed into the underworld by the falling sky, and turned into sharp-toothed cannibals.

THE HOMESICK GHOSTS

In a traditional story, a group of homesick ghosts missed their living families so much that they decided to return to earth. They climbed down a vine through a hole in the sky and traveled back to their village, building shelters, putting up hammocks, and embracing their loved ones. But the ghosts were startled by the shrieking of a tinamou bird, and rushed back to the vine, climbing into the sky. As they fled, a parrot flew after them and, with a snap of its beak, sliced through the vine. It fell to the ground, cutting off the ladder from earth to heaven, so the ghosts could never visit again. One day, however, the families will be reunited in the House of Souls in the sky.

Mountain peaks were said to be sacred portals to the heavens, while caves and springs linked our world to the underworld.

THREE PACHAS: THE WORLDS OF THE INCAS

In the fifteenth century, the Incas ruled over a large empire that stretched north to south along the Andes Mountains. The Inca people saw the world as divided into three layers: Hanan Pacha (the world above), Kay Pacha (our world), and Ukhu Pacha (the world below). The Incas believed that after a person died, their spirit might inhabit any of these three realms. Spirits of the dead might travel to the skies or down to the world below—or they might remain in this world, Kay Pacha, in the form of a plant or animal, staying close to their loved ones.

In Inca artwork, condors were symbols of the heavens, pumas represented the earth, and snakes symbolized the underworld.

Hanan Pacha was the realm of the sun god Inti, the moon goddess Mama Quilla, and Illapa, god of thunder and lightning.

Amaru was a huge serpent thought to live in Ukhu Pacha.

The World Below

The underworld of Ukhu Pacha was a place of both death and new life. It was a sacred realm inhabited by the supay, the shadows of the dead, and by the powerful fertility goddess Pachamama. The Incas treated the land with care. Whenever they disturbed this lower world, for example by tilling the soil, they made offerings to appease Pachamama.

Life After Death

The Incas believed that life carried on after death, and that deceased spirits watched over the living. In turn, the dead needed to be looked after. When an important person died, their body was mummified (preserved and dried), usually in an upright sitting position. People often visited their dead relations, bringing offerings and asking for advice. Sometimes, priests spoke on behalf of the mummies. The bodies of dead emperors received luxury treatment. When an emperor died, his mummy remained in the palace, dressed in lavish clothes. He was tended by servants, brought food every day, and even provided with entertainment!

BAGANA: Volcano afterworld for people from the nearby Shortland Islands

KIBU: Island of ghosts

PAPUA NEW GUINEA

HIYOYOA: Underwater paradise gardens

BARALKU: Faraway island of the dead for Australia's Yolngu people

TRAIL OF STARS: For some Aboriginal Australians, the Milky Way was the pathway taken by the spirits of the dead

INDIAN OCEAN

AUSTRALIA

WANDANGGANGURA: In the stories of the Wiradjuri people, the dead travel to this place beyond the clouds

BANOI: Souls leaping across the water to this Vanuatu paradise might get bitten by a shark on the way

FIJI

VANUATU

KANGAROO ISLAND: Known as Karta Pintingga, the "Island of the Dead," to local Aboriginal people

COOLANGATTA MOUNTAIN: Place from where souls depart to the land of the dead, according to local legend

RAROHENGA: In the Māori tradition, the dead dwell in this peaceful underworld ruled by the goddess of death, Hine-nui-te-pō

NEW ZEALAND

Lua-o-Milu:
The Hawaiian land of the dead

HAWAI'I, USA

PACIAC
OCEAN

Pulotu: Legendary island in the west where the souls of Samoan chiefs were believed to end up

SAMOA

Bulu: World of spirits in Fijian mythology, sometimes reached via a waterfall

Vatea's Sunny Land:
On the Cook Islands, the dead were thought to travel to the heavenly world of the sky god

COOK ISLANDS

Cape Reinga: Māori spirits are thought to depart for the afterlife from this northernmost tip of New Zealand

Australasia & Oceania

Australasia and Oceania are home to thousands of islands that lie scattered across the Pacific. Through history, people from this region pictured the land of the dead in many different ways: some saw it as a beautiful underwater garden, while others believed it was a distant island far to the west, beyond the setting sun. According to some, the spirits of the dead traveled to the next world by boat; others thought that journeying souls would leap from a high clifftop to reach their final destination.

KIBU: ISLAND OF GHOSTS

To the north of Australia lie the islands of the Torres Strait, where indigenous peoples have lived for thousands of years. In the past, the people of the western Torres Strait believed that at the edge of the world, where the setting sun met the horizon, lay an island of ghosts. This place, named Kibu, was thought to be the final destination for the spirits of the dead. When a spirit left a person's body, it would travel west across the ocean to Kibu, carried by the winds.

LIFE ON KIBU

For the western islanders, a mari was a spirit that hadn't yet passed to the other side. When a mari arrived at Kibu, it was thought to be met by the ghost of a friend, who took it somewhere quiet until the rising of the next new moon. Then, the friend would introduce the mari to other ghosts, who gathered around to hit the new arrival on the head with a stone club. This was believed to turn it from a mari into a markai: from a wispy spirit into a more substantial ghost.

The full name of Kibu is "Kibukuth," which means "Horizon's End."

HONORING THE DEAD

On the island of Mabuiag, several months after someone had died, the people often held a ceremony to remember them. In this "death dance," a performer would act the part of the departed person's ghost. Masks made of turtle shells were sometimes worn in these ceremonies to honor the dead and help them travel to Kibu.

BECOMING A GHOST

Some thought the markai of Kibu took the form of large bats, which lived in the treetops, chirping and twittering. Others, however, believed that the markai looked like people, and carried on in much the same way as the living did: spear-fishing, hunting turtles, and dancing on the beach when twilight fell. The living could never reach Kibu, but ghosts might choose to return to the world of the living for a short visit, once more crossing the line between life and death.

Throughout history, many different cultures across the world have told stories about far-away islands of the dead.

PAPUA NEW GUINEA

TORRES STRAIT ISLANDS

AUSTRALIA

HIYOYOA: UNDERWATER GARDENS OF THE DEAD

Beneath the turquoise seas of Milne Bay, Papua New Guinea, is said to lie a realm of beautiful underwater gardens that are home to the souls of the dead. In the traditional beliefs of the Wagawaga people from eastern Papua New Guinea, when someone dies, their spirit—which is called the arugo—leaves the body and travels to Hiyoyoa: a tranquil, sun-dappled underwater world. Here, they spend a peaceful afterlife tending quietly to their gardens.

When it was nighttime in the living world, it was daytime in Hiyoyoa, and vice versa.

LORD OF THE DEAD

When a new soul arrives in this colorful coral kingdom, it is greeted by Tumudurere, the larger-than-life lord of the dead. He lives in a house on a hill, overlooking his underwater domain, with his wife and children. As each soul enters Hiyoyoa, he welcomes them and shows them where to make their garden.

VISITING HIYOYOA

It's said that the souls of the dead cannot leave Hiyoyoa, but the living can make visits. Sometimes, if you dive deep enough, you might catch a glimpse of its delightful gardens. Once, a man named Wakuri claimed he had visited the land of the dead many times—or at least, his spirit had, while his body remained in a trance on dry land. Wakuri was careful not to eat the food in Hiyoyoa, for fear that this would prevent him from ever returning to the world of the living.

WAGAWAGA HOMELAND

PAPUA NEW GUINEA

Certain flowers in Papua New Guinea were said to have been grown from underwater plants brought back by visitors to the land of the dead.

LUA-O-MILU: THE HAWAIIAN LAND OF THE DEAD

On the islands of Hawai'i, there were once many different beliefs about the afterlife, but they all shared the idea that the soul lived on after the death of the body. The spirits of people who worshipped the sun god might travel to a heaven beyond the clouds, while the bones of others might be cast into a volcano so they could be close to the fire goddess, Pele. Some believed that an island of the dead lay far to the west, while others told of a shadowy underworld named Lua-o-Milu.

Often taking the form of animals, such as owls or sharks, the 'aumakua were spirits that protected the souls of the dead, leading them to the next world.

In the traditions of many Pacific islands, the souls of the dead departed from a high clifftop overlooking the sea.

THE PIT OF MILU

Some said that the underworld was divided into an upper kingdom ruled by the sky god Wakea, and a lower world ruled by Milu, the god of the dead. The upper kingdom, for those who had led good lives, was peaceful and comfortable, but Lua-o-Milu (the "Pit of Milu") was dark and miserable. In this noisy, chaotic world, the spirits of the dead were forced to eat lizards and butterflies. However, in other versions of the story, Lua-o-Milu did not seem like such a terrible place to end up: souls were said to spend their time playing games and sports, and feasting on plentiful food.

Milu, god of the dead, was once a chief on earth, who was punished for his disobedience to the gods by being swept down to the underworld.

Some unfortunate souls might be abandoned by the 'aumakua and left to wander, lonely and forlorn.

THE LEAPING PLACE

To reach Lua-o-Milu, it was said that the spirits of the dead must travel to a high clifftop, from where they would make their final leap to the underworld. Every region had its own "leina a ka 'uhane," which means "the leaping place of the soul." On the island of Maui, for example, the jumping-off point was said to be at Kahakuloa Head, while on Oahu it was at Ka'ena Point. At these sacred places, the souls might cling to certain trees before the last leap: sometimes a candle-nut tree; sometimes a breadfruit tree. It was said that animal spirit guardians called 'aumakua might gather around the tree, ready to help guide souls to the afterlife.

Each Hawaiian island had its own leaping place for departing souls. Hawai'i, the Big Island, had several, some of which are shown here.

WAIPI'O VALLEY

CAPE KUMUKAHI

HAWAI'I

SOUTH POINT

Afterword

And so at last we come to the end of our journey through the afterlife. We've traveled from the golden halls of Viking Valhalla and the eternal summer of the Celtic Otherworld to the dangerous labyrinth of the Egyptian nether-realm and the celestial cities of the Hindu heavens. You have seen how the question of what happens to us when we die has been asked, and answered, by our ancestors.

Yet the afterlife is the greatest unknown: the unanswerable question. Because no traveler has ever returned from the dead, it's impossible for us to know what lies beyond the world of the living. Some believe that the answers are out of reach, or that what happens after death is in the hands of God, or many gods. Ultimately, the afterlife will remain a mystery. When thinking about death, many find comfort in the words of the poet Rabindranath Tagore, who said, "Death is not extinguishing the light; it is only putting out the lamp because the dawn has come."

If you don't believe in a god, or that people have
souls, there is another way to think about death: as part of
the circle of life to which we all belong. All living things, from people
and animals to trees and flowers, are made of the same elements—
the building blocks of life. When a living thing dies, it stops breathing,
moving, and feeling, and its body starts to decompose. This means that the
particles break down and are released back into the air and soil. Eventually,
the body disappears, but the building blocks that made it don't vanish.
They will be recycled, becoming part of something else, a new living
thing—perhaps a bird, a butterfly, or a flower. Nothing lives forever, but
the building blocks of each living thing will endure, as part of the
constant, never-ending circle of life. In many ways, then, death
is not only an ending—it is also a beginning.

GLOSSARY

ABYSS — A bottomless pit

AFTERLIFE — In some religions, the place people go after they die

ANCESTOR — A relative who lived a long time ago

ARCHAEOLOGIST — Someone who studies historical remains such as ruins

BARREN — Used to describe land that is not able to grow plants

BREASTPLATE — A piece of armor that covers the chest

CELESTIAL — To do with the sky or the idea of heaven

DECEASED — No longer living, or someone who has recently died

DEMON — An evil spirit or devil

ETERNITY — Endless life after death, or endless time

FOLKLORE — Traditional beliefs, stories, and customs

FUNERAL — A ceremony held after someone has died

HEAVEN — In some religions, a peaceful place where good people go when they die

HELL — In some religions, a frightening place where bad or evil people are thought to be punished after they die

HIEROGLYPH — A picture that represents a word or sound in ancient Egyptian writing

IMMORTAL — Living forever

INDIGENOUS — Directly descended from the earliest inhabitants of a particular place

KARMA — In Buddhism and Hinduism, the force created by a person's good or bad actions

MEAD — An alcoholic drink made from honey

MEAD HALL — A place for community gatherings in historic Scandinavian and Northern European cultures

MEDIEVAL — The period of time between the fifth and fifteenth centuries

MYTHOLOGY — A collection of traditional stories from a particular culture

OMEN	An event regarded as a sign of what is going to happen	SHRINE	A religious space
OTHERWORLD	A world beyond death or earthly reality	SINKHOLE	A hole in the ground, formed when the land collapses away
PAPYRUS	A material made from a water plant, used for writing on	SOUL	The non-physical or spiritual part of a person that many religions believe lives on after death
PHANTOM	The spirit of a dead person or animal that is thought to appear to the living	TEMPLE	A building used for the worship of a god or gods
REALM	A place or territory, usually ruled by someone	TOLL	Money you have to pay to cross something such as a bridge or river
REINCARNATION	The belief that after death the soul is born again in another body	UNDERWORLD	The home of the dead, imagined as being under the earth
SACRED	Regarded with great respect by a particular religion or group	VIRTUOUS	Having or showing moral goodness

BOOKS THAT HAVE INSPIRED US

The Children's Illustrated Encyclopedia of Heaven
Anita Ganeri (Element Children's Books, 1999)

Death and the Afterlife
Clifford A. Pickover (Sterling, 2015)

The Devil's Atlas: An Explorer's Guide to Heavens, Hells and Afterworlds
Edward Brooke-Hitching (Simon & Schuster, 2021)

Fox: A Circle of Life Story
Isabel Thomas (Bloomsbury, 2020)

The Un-Discovered Islands
Malachy Tallack (Polygon, 2016)

INDEX

A

A'aru, Field of Reeds 32, 33
Aboriginal beliefs 80, 81
Adlivun 58, 64–65
Ahura Mazda 54, 55
Alaska 65
Algonquian beliefs 59
Allah 46
All Hallows' Eve 28
Amaravati 49
Amaterasu 57
Amazon rainforest 76
Amokye 38, 39
ancestors 18, 34, 56, 62, 63, 71, 77
angels 20, 21, 23, 46, 54
animals 17, 23, 31, 36, 49, 50, 51, 57, 64, 65, 72, 73, 75, 77, 79, 86, 87
 dogs and hounds 15, 17, 28, 29, 32, 33, 36, 54, 68
 horses 16, 17, 28, 29, 53
 serpents and snakes 22, 32, 54, 69, 79
Ankou, the 27
Annwn 24
Arabian Peninsula 46
Arctic, the 64, 65
Asamando 30, 38–39
Ashanti beliefs 30, 38–39
Asto Vidatu 55
'aumakua 86, 87
Australia 60, 80, 81, 82, 83
Avalon 24
Aztec beliefs 58, 68–69, 72

B

Bag Noz, the 12, 26–27
Bambara beliefs 30
Bambuti beliefs 31
Baralku 80
Baron Samedi 67
Bel ze 72, 73
Berin 66
Bible, the 20, 21, 22, 40
birds 16, 18, 45, 47, 57, 68, 69, 75, 77, 79, 86
bird-women 19
boats 26–27, 32, 64, 71, 74–75, 80
Book of the Dead, the 33
Borneo beliefs 41
Brahman 49
Breton folklore 12, 26–27
bridges 40, 45, 54–55, 59, 65
Britain 12, 24, 26, 28
Brittany 26
Buddha, the 51
Buddhism 41, 50, 51
burial 15, 17, 24, 33, 38, 39, 52, 53, 56, 61, 63, 68, 70, 72

C

Caleuche, El/the 70, 74–75
Canada 59, 64, 65
Celtic mythology 12, 24–25
Chagga beliefs 31
Cherokee folklore 59
Cheyenne beliefs 61
Chile 70, 74, 75
Chiloé 74, 75
China 41, 52, 53
Chinese beliefs, ancient 53
Chinook folklore 58
Chinvat Bridge 40, 54–55
Christianity 13, 17, 20, 21, 23, 44, 48, 66
Citipati, the 50
Cook Islands beliefs 81

D

Dahomey 66
Dante 20, 22
Darvaza Crater 40
Day of the Dead 58, 59, 69
Demeter 15
demons 12, 22, 23, 29, 43, 44, 51, 54, 55, 70, 72,
Devil, the 23, 29, 44
Donn 25
Duat 31, 32–33

E

Egypt 31, 32
Egyptian beliefs, ancient 30, 31, 32–33
Eklutna spirit houses 58
English folklore 24, 29
enslavement 35, 66
Ereshkigal 43
Erlik 44
Ethiopia 31

F

Fengdu 41
Fijian mythology 81
Finnish mythology 13
food and feasting 16, 17, 22, 36, 42, 61, 63, 77, 78, 84, 86
France 12, 26, 28
funerals 15, 17, 37, 68

G

gardens 13, 18–19, 40, 46–47, 49, 80, 81, 84–85
gates 13, 15, 19, 21, 22–23, 32, 40, 42, 43, 59, 66–67
Gates of Guinee 59, 66–67
Germanic beliefs 28, 29
Ghana 30, 38
ghosts 28–29, 50, 60, 70, 74–75, 77, 80, 82–83
 see also Fengdu *and* Kibu
God (Christianity) 20, 21, 23
Greece 14
Greek beliefs, ancient 12, 13, 14–15
Greenland 64, 65

Grimm, Jacob 28
Gros Ventre beliefs 59
Guanche beliefs 12
Guatemala 72, 73
Gwyn ap Nudd 29

H

Hades 12, 13, 14–15
Haiti 66
Hawai'i 86, 87
Hawaiian beliefs 81, 86–87
Heaven (Christian) 20, 21, 23
Hedu 71, 76–77
Hel (Norse) 17
Hell (Christian) 13, 17, 22–23
Herne the Hunter 29
Hihankara, the Owl Maker 60
Hinduism 40, 48, 49, 50, 51
Hiyoyoa 81, 84–85
House of Lies, the 54
House of Song, the 54, 55

I

Inanna 43
Inca beliefs 71, 78–79
India 41, 49, 50
Indigenous American beliefs 58, 60, 61, 62, 63
Indra 48, 49
Inuit beliefs 59, 64–65
Ireland 12, 24
Irish mythology 12, 24, 25
Irkalla 40, 42–43
Islam 40, 46–47, 48, 55
Itsukushima Shrine 56

J

Jacob's Ladder 13, 20–21
Jahannam 46
Jannah 40, 46–47
Japan 41, 56, 57
judgment 32, 33, 46, 54

K

Kakuriyo 41, 56–57
Kalapalo beliefs 71
Kalunga Line, the 30, 34–35
kami 57
Kangaroo Island 80
karma 49, 50
Kibu 80, 82–83
koko, the 62, 63
Kongo 34, 35
Kongolese beliefs 34–35
Kormos 45
Kothluwalawa 58, 62–63
Kwasi Benefo 38, 39

L

Lakota beliefs 59, 60–61
Lua-o-Milu 81, 86–87

M

Mag Mell	24
Māori beliefs	81
Maya beliefs	70, 72–73
Mecca	46
mermaids	74
Mesopotamia	40, 42
Mexico	58, 59, 68, 72, 73
Mictlan	58, 68–69
Mictlantecuhtli and Mictecacihuatl	69
Milky Way, the	60, 61, 81
Milu	86
Moche Pyramids	70
Mongolia	41, 45
Mongolian beliefs	41, 44–45
moon	45, 64, 76, 78, 82
mountains	12, 40, 44, 45, 56, 57, 58, 68, 78
Alborz Mountains	55
Andes	79
Burkhan Khaldun	45
Ceahlau Massif	13
Coolangatta Mountain	81
Harburz	55
Himalayas	49
Kailash, Mount	41
Kilimanjaro	31
Kunlun, Mount	41
Meru, Mount	41, 48, 49
Roraima, Mount	71
Zagros Mountains	42
see also volcanoes	
Muhammad	46
mummification	33, 78

N

Nepal	41, 51
New Mexico	62
New Orleans	66, 67
New Zealand	81
Nez Perce folklore	58
Norse mythology	16, 29
Nuer mythology	31

O

oceans and seas	24, 25, 26, 30, 34, 35, 42, 49, 56, 64, 65, 74, 75, 82, 84, 86
Odin	16, 29
Ojibwe folklore	59
Oromo beliefs	31
Otherworld, the (Celtic)	12, 24–25

P

Papua New Guinea	83, 84
Paris Catacombs	12
Pemon beliefs	71
Persephone	15
Pluto's Gate	40
Popol Vuh, the	73
Procopius	26
punishment	15, 22, 50, 51

Q

Qin Shi Huang	52, 53
Quran, the	46

R

rebirth	30, 48, 49, 50, 67, 72
reincarnation	*see* rebirth
rivers	14, 30, 32, 35, 39, 46, 47, 49, 57, 63, 68, 72, 73
Nile	32
Sanzu	41
Styx	14, 15
Zuni	62, 63
Romanian folklore	13

S

Samhain, Feast of	25
Samoan beliefs	81
Scandinavia	16
Scot, Michael	23
seas	*see* oceans
seasons	15, 18, 24
Sedna	64, 65
Seminole beliefs	61
Shachi	48
Sheol	40
Shinto	41, 56, 57
ships	*see* boats
Shona beliefs	31
Shortland Islands	81
Sima Qian	53
Sisyphus	15
skeletons	12, 27, 50, 67, 69
Slavic beliefs and people	13, 18
stars	20, 30, 45, 58, 59, 60–61, 76, 81
Sumerian beliefs	40, 42–43
sun	57, 59, 68, 72, 76, 78, 86
rising	18, 32
setting	24, 25, 34, 80, 82
Svarga	40, 48–49
Swahili mythology	31

T

Tamag	41, 44–45
Taoism	41
Terracotta Army, the	41, 52–53
Thompson River beliefs	58
Three Pachas, the	71, 78–79
thunder and lightning	29, 48, 77, 78
Tir na nÓg	24, 25
Tlingit folklore	58
Torres Strait Islander beliefs	82–83
Trail of Spirits, the	59, 60–61
trees	15, 18, 19, 24, 39, 46, 57, 61, 72, 77, 87
Tumudurere	84
Turkic beliefs	41, 44–45

U

Uçmag	41, 44–45
Uganda	36
Ughoton	31
Ülgen	44, 45
Uncama	36–37

V

Valhalla	12, 13, 16–17
Valkyries, the	16
Vanuatu	81
Viking beliefs	12, 13, 16–17
volcanoes	12, 86
Bagana	81
Erta Ale (lava lake)	31
Hekla Volcano	12
Masaya Volcano	70
Teide, Mount	12
Voudou	59, 66–67
Vyraj	13, 18–19

W

Wagawaga beliefs	84–85
Wanagi Makoce	61
Wang Saen Suk	41
Welsh folklore	24, 29
Wild Hunt, the	28–29
Winnebago beliefs	59
Wiradjuri beliefs	81

X

Xibalba	70, 72–73

Y

Yama	41, 50, 51
Yanomami beliefs	70, 71, 76–77
Yayik	44
Yayutshis	44, 45
Yolngu beliefs	80
Yucatán Peninsula	73
Yule	28

Z

zombis	67
Zoroastrianism	40, 54
Zulu beliefs	31, 36–37
Zuni beliefs	58, 62–63

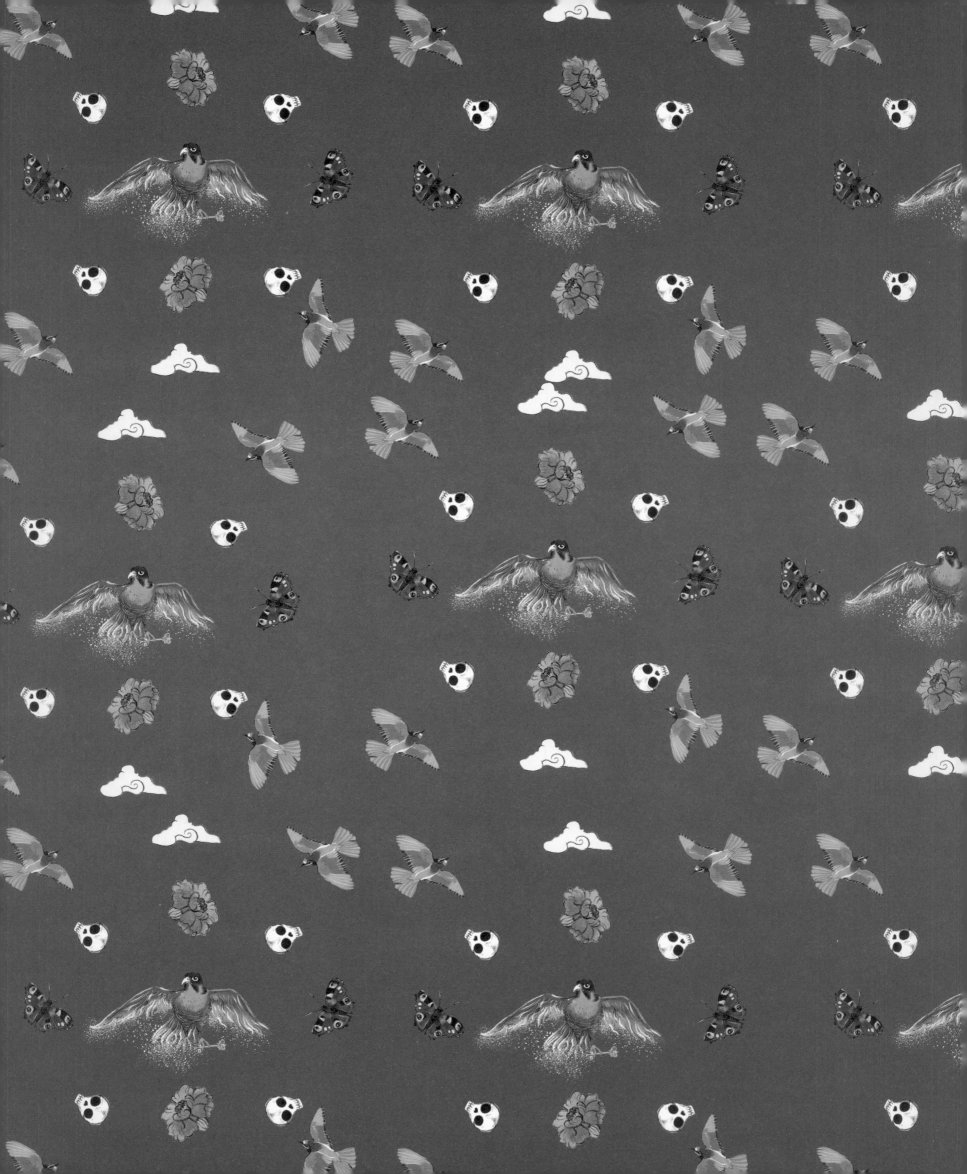